The Startup Symphony

Orchestrating Business Brilliance

Natalie Blythe

Foreword

Welcome to your path of entrepreneurial discovery and development. This book will take you on a transforming journey through the crucial aspects that lead to the creation of a successful company. It is a journey that spans the width and depth of entrepreneurship, from establishing the groundwork to reaching new heights, and from overcoming obstacles to seizing chances.

These chapters provide a wealth of knowledge, ideas, and practical techniques that have been painstakingly created to take you through the exciting and often difficult journey of entrepreneurship. Each chapter delves into a vital component of starting a business, presenting it with clarity and purpose while kindling your entrepreneurial spirit.

As you read the pages, you'll learn the fundamentals of entrepreneurship, beginning with the critical work of creating your vision and goal. You will understand the value of performing extensive market research and studying the competitive environment in order to identify and attract your target clients. You will then master the skill of creating a value proposition that captivates and compels, setting the framework for success.

A great business strategy serves as your compass, giving a path for navigating the entrepreneurial terrain. You will learn about establishing your company concept, setting realistic goals, and developing a financial strategy to fuel your desires. Along the way, you'll learn how to identify risks and adopt risk-mitigation measures, allowing your business to grow.

A successful venture cannot survive without a strong team. You will learn how to define roles and duties, recruit top personnel, develop cooperation, and build effective leadership and communication channels on these pages. You establish a culture that fosters creativity and moves your business ahead by cultivating employee enthusiasm and engagement.

The funding of your firm is a critical stage in your entrepreneurial journey. You will examine numerous financing possibilities and learn the art of presenting and structuring proposals that attract the proper investors, from self-funding and bootstrapping to pursuing angel investors and venture capitalists. With a strong foundation in place, you will begin on the thrilling path of product development and launch, learning the complexities of prototyping, testing, incorporating user input, and designing successful releases that leave an indelible impact.

As you identify your target market, construct a compelling brand identity, develop thorough marketing plans, and apply digital marketing techniques that position your business for success, marketing and growth strategies will become your valued partners. You will learn the skill of assessing and optimizing growth, ensuring that your initiatives are in line with business objectives.

Managing operations, scaling up, and negotiating obstacles will put your entrepreneurial skills to the test. However, armed with this knowledge, you will be able to develop effective processes and systems, manage cash flow and resources, streamline supply chain and logistics, and analyze and change business performance. You will learn how to negotiate uncertainty, adapt to changing market circumstances, overcome competition and disruption, and develop resilience based on failure lessons.

As you progress through the book, you will learn about the critical principles of customer acquisition and retention tactics, innovation, continuous improvement, market expansion, and the formation of strategic partnerships and alliances. These chapters will teach you how to acquire new consumers, establish steadfast loyalty, improve the customer experience, promote an innovative culture, adopt lean and agile approaches, and design market expansion plans.

It is now time to immerse yourself in the transforming experience that awaits you. These pages' knowledge and insight will enable you to take brave moves, make educated judgments, and determine the fate of your business. Allow this book to be your guide, companion, and source of inspiration as you pursue business success.

Embrace the journey, the difficulties, and the endless opportunities that await you. Your entrepreneurial journey has just begun.

Summary

Chapter 1: Laying the Foundation

Defining Your Vision and Mission

Building a business needs a clear vision and goal to guide the path and purpose of your organization. Here's a step-by-step process to creating your vision and mission statement:

Recognize the Difference:

Your vision is a long-term, aspirational statement that represents the future condition or influence of your business. It offers a general feeling of direction and inspiration.

Mission: Your mission is a succinct statement that outlines the goal of your business, its target audience, and how you intend to offer value. It is present-oriented and outlines what your startup does.

Consider Your Values:

Think about the essential values that will govern your startup's activities and decisions. What are your guiding values and beliefs? Take the time to discover these values since they will have an impact on your vision and goal.

Create Your Vision:

Consider the influence you want your business to have in the future. Consider the following questions: What problem do you wish to solve?

What kind of constructive change do you wish to see in the world?

In the long term, how do you want your startup to be perceived?

Create a clear, inspirational, and short statement that communicates the ultimate aim of your firm.

Make Your Mission:

Take into account your intended audience or consumers. Who exactly are they? What are you addressing in terms of needs or pain points?

Describe how your startup addresses these needs or solves the problem. How do you intend to provide value?

Keep your mission statement short, to the point, and action-oriented. It should be memorable and simple to comprehend.

Align Vision and Mission:

Make sure your vision and mission statements are in sync. They should work together to provide your startup a feeling of purpose and direction.

Examine both statements concurrently and make any required changes to guarantee consistency.

Iterate and refine:

As your business develops and reacts to market changes, your vision and purpose may shift. Revisit and improve them on a regular basis to ensure they stay current and inspirational.

To obtain multiple viewpoints and insights, solicit input from stakeholders, workers, and consumers. This input may be used to strengthen your vision and mission statements.

Internal and external communication:

Share your vision and mission with your team members to develop a feeling of purpose and align everyone around common goals.

Externally, communicate your vision and mission through your website, marketing materials, and other avenues of contact. It explains to potential clients, investors, and partners what your business stands for and what you hope to achieve.

Be Specific and Unique:

Your vision and goal should represent your startup's distinct value offer. Avoid broad comments that might apply to any business. Instead, concentrate on what distinguishes your business and how it may make a significant effect.

Inspire and Motivate Your Team and Stakeholders:

Your vision should inspire and motivate both your team and your stakeholders. It should instill a feeling of purpose and enthusiasm for the future. Use language that piques the reader's interest and elicits strong emotions.

Ensure Feasibility:

Your vision should be both ambitious and feasible. Consider the resources, competencies, and market circumstances needed to bring your idea to fruition. Find a happy medium between ambition and reality.

Keep it Simple:

Your vision and purpose statements should be brief and easy to understand. Avoid using too much jargon or sophisticated terminology, which may confuse or alienate your readers. Aim for simplicity and clarity.

Examine and align with the business strategy:

Make sure your vision and purpose are in sync with your entire business plan. They should be in line with your target market, product or service offers, and expansion objectives. This guarantees that all aspects of your startup are heading in the same direction.

Highlight the beneficial influence your business can have on consumers, society, or the industry. Outline the benefits and results that your products or services may provide. This aids in the development of a compelling narrative for your company.

Review and Re-evaluate:

As your business grows, review and analyze your vision and purpose on a frequent basis. Are they still relevant and in line with your objectives? Consider if changes in the market or internal circumstances necessitate revisions to your financial statements.

Inspire Buy-In:

Your vision and goal should resonate not only with your staff, but also with investors, partners, and consumers. Communicate them effectively to generate excitement and support for your business.

Remember that your vision and mission statements should act as a guide for the path of your business. They give clarity, purpose, and motivation to drive decision-making, attract top people, and distinguish your firm in a competitive industry. As you mature, evaluate and adjust them on a regular basis to ensure they stay consistent with your basic beliefs and ambitions.

Conducting Market Research

Market research is an important phase in the company development process since it helps you understand your target market, competitors, and industry trends. Here's a step-by-step approach to market research:

Define your research goals:

Begin by clearly outlining your goals for doing market research. Determine the precise questions you want to answer and the data you need to collect. This will direct your research.

Determine your target market:

Determine the precise consumer or market group that you want to serve. Define your target audience's qualities, demographics, and behaviors. This allows you to properly target your research efforts.

Decide on a research methodology:

Based on your objectives and available resources, select the suitable research methodology. Surveys, interviews, focus groups, observational studies, and secondary data analysis are all common methodologies.

Collect primary data:

If you're doing primary research, create questionnaires or interview questions that will collect the essential information. To collect data from your target audience, use online survey tools, face-to-face interviews, or phone interviews.

Gather existing information from trustworthy sources such as industry reports, market studies, government publications, and academic research. This assists you in comprehending the larger market landscape, industry trends, and competition analyses.

Examine the data:

Prepare your data for analysis by cleaning and organizing it. Search for patterns, trends, and insights that can help you make business decisions. If required, use statistical tools or software to assist with data analysis.

Recognize the demands and preferences of your customers:

Determine your target clients' needs, pain spots, and preferences. Analyze their behavior, purchase patterns, and comments to learn how your product or service may best meet their requirements.

Assess the competition:

Perform a competitive study to learn about your direct and indirect rivals. Determine their strengths and limitations, as well as their market positioning, pricing, and marketing tactics. This study assists you in differentiating your business and identifying growth prospects.

Keep up with industry trends:

Keep an eye on industry developments, new technology, laws, and customer behavior. Keep up to date on developments that may have an influence on the growth of your business and adjust your plans accordingly.

Interpret and apply the results:

Convert the study findings into useful insights. Utilize the data to improve your company's strategy, product development, marketing approach, and consumer interaction. In order to make educated judgments, incorporate the study findings.

Iterate and keep researching:

Market research is a continuous activity. Gather client input on a regular basis, watch market developments, and keep an eye on competitors. Keep your research up to date in order to stay ahead of the competition and react to changing market conditions.

Employ a mix of qualitative and quantitative research:

Interviews and focus groups, for example, can give in-depth insights into consumer motives, preferences, and problem issues. Quantitative research methods, such as surveys and data analysis, enable you to collect data on a broad scale and assess trends and patterns over a bigger sample size. Use these tactics to acquire a thorough grasp of your market.

Consider primary research strategies:

Investigate numerous primary research methodologies based on your study objectives and target audience. Online surveys, face-to-face interviews, usability testing, and consumer observation might all be used. Choose approaches that allow you to engage with your target market directly and gain particular information.

Utilize secondary research sources:

Secondary research delivers current data and insights gathered by others. Examine market research papers, competition websites, trade journals, and government databases. This data may provide you with a more comprehensive view of market trends, customer behavior, and industry dynamics.

Pilot testing can help you validate assumptions about your target market or product. This might include releasing a limited-edition version of your product or testing your marketing strategy to assess customer interest and get feedback prior to a full release.

Engage with your target audience:

Throughout the research process, actively engage with your target audience. Collect comments, conduct surveys, and promote open discourse. This interaction not only gives useful information but also aids in the development of relationships and the formation of a community around your business.

Objectively analyze and evaluate data:

Avoid confirmation bias by approaching data analysis with an open mind. In the data, look for trends, patterns, and outliers. To gain useful insights, use visualization tools and statistical approaches. Interpret the information objectively and make data-driven judgments.

Consult with industry experts, consultants, or mentors who have expertise in your target market or sector to acquire professional perspectives and guidance. They can provide insights, assistance, and validation for your research strategy. Their knowledge and experience can give useful views and assist you in making sound judgments.

Keep privacy and ethical factors in mind:

When gathering and analyzing data, ensure that privacy legislation and ethical norms are followed. Respect the privacy of participants, acquire informed consent, and anonymize data as needed. It is critical to safeguard participants' anonymity and rights.

Iterate and update your research:

Market research is a process that is iterative. As your business grows, examine and update your research on a regular basis. Maintain a keen awareness of shifting market dynamics, client demands, and industry trends. Reassess your research strategies on a regular basis and change as needed.

Market research offers you with data-driven insights and expertise that may help influence your startup's strategy, product development, marketing efforts, and overall decision-making. You may boost your chances of success and establish a company that effectively solves consumer requirements and grabs market opportunities by investing in extensive and continuing research.

Analyzing the Competitive Landscape

Analyzing the competitive environment is an important part of conducting market research for your firm. It assists you in understanding your rivals' strengths and shortcomings, as well as how your business might differentiate itself. Here's how to analyze the competitive landscape step by step:

Determine who your direct and indirect rivals are: Determine your primary rivals in your target market. Direct rivals provide comparable goods or services to the same client base. Indirect rivals handle comparable client demands while offering different solutions or operating in separate sectors.

Collect information on your competitors:

Perform extensive study on each rival. Investigate their websites, social media accounts, marketing materials, and other publicly available information. Examine their product offers, pricing strategy, target market, distribution routes, and value proposition.

Consider their advantages and disadvantages:

Determine each competitor's strengths and competitive advantages. Consider their brand reputation, market share, client base, technological skills, and unique selling qualities.

Analyze their vulnerabilities as well as places where your startup may have a competitive advantage. This might include product gaps, bad customer service, a restricted geographical reach, or obsolete technology.

Assess their market positioning:

Determine how your rivals are positioned in the market. Are they primarily interested in low-cost offers, luxury items, specialized markets, or creative solutions? Understanding their positioning allows you to uncover chances for differentiating your firm and addressing unmet client demands.

Examine their marketing and sales strategies: Examine how your rivals promote and sell their goods or services. Examine their website, advertising efforts, content marketing, social media participation, and distribution routes. Determine any unique marketing approaches or strategies they use.

Consider the following consumer comments and reviews:

Examine consumer reviews, testimonials, and comments on review sites, social media, and industry-specific forums. Understand what customers like about your rivals' offerings and where they fall short. This assists you in identifying possible areas for development in your own startup.

Analyze price tactics:

Investigate your rivals' pricing methods. Examine their price structures, discounts, bundling possibilities, and subscription programs. Determine whether they are concerned with cost leadership, distinctiveness, or value-based pricing. Consider how your pricing approach might provide you a competitive advantage.

Determine probable access barriers:

Determine the obstacles in your business or market. High financial needs, strong client loyalty to current brands, onerous laws, or proprietary technologies might all be examples. Examine how these obstacles affect the competitive environment and look for ways to overcome or use them.

Keep an eye on industry trends and developments: Stay up to date on developing trends, technologies, and breakthroughs in your sector. Examine how your rivals are adjusting to or leading these developments. Determine areas where you can innovate or differentiate yourself to acquire a competitive advantage.

Compile findings and create a competitive strategy:

Consolidate the information acquired and describe your competitive landscape research. Determine the important insights, opportunities, and dangers affecting your startup.

Develop a competitive strategy based on your study that defines how your startup will differentiate itself, capitalize on opportunities, and answer consumer requirements better than rivals.

Keep in mind that assessing the competitive environment is a continuous activity. Monitor your competition often and adjust your strategy as market conditions change. Understanding your rivals' strengths, limitations, and positioning allows you to make educated decisions and design tactics that will provide your firm a market edge.

Identifying Target Customers

Identifying your target clients is a critical phase in the development of a company. Understanding who your consumers are and what they require helps you to successfully personalize your products, services, and marketing techniques. Here's a step-by-step procedure for determining your target customers:

Define Your Service or Product:
Clearly state the problem that your product or service addresses or the value that it delivers. Understand its distinct features and benefits, as well as how it differs from existing options. This clarity will aid in the identification of your target consumer.

Gather facts and insights about your industry, market trends, and possible consumer categories by conducting market research. Investigate market studies, trade journals, and internet resources. Determine the size, development potential, and characteristics of various client groups that are compatible with your product or service.

Analyze Existing consumers:

Examine your existing consumers' demographics, activities, preferences, and purchasing patterns. Examine your existing consumer base for commonalities such as age, gender, region, career, interests, or demands. This study might give preliminary information about your potential clients.

Create Customer Personas:

Based on your research and analysis, create complete profiles of your ideal customers. Customer personas are fictitious representations of your target customers' demographics, motivations, objectives, issues, and preferences. Make use of these characters to better empathize and understand your target audience.

Divide your target market into discrete divisions based on common features, demands, or habits. Consider demographics, psychographics, region, industry, firm size, or purchasing power. This segmentation enables you to concentrate your efforts on the most important consumer segments.

Prioritize Target Segments:
Assess and rank the market segments you've found based on their attractiveness and fit with your startup's skills and ambitions. Consider market size, future growth, competition intensity, alignment with your value offer, and resource needs.

improve Your Customer Profiles:
As you obtain new information and insights, continue to improve and update your customer personas and market segments. Stay receptive to client input, perform surveys or interviews, and watch market developments to verify the accuracy and relevancy of your target customer profiles.

Test and validate your assumptions about your target clients by connecting with them firsthand. To acquire feedback and confirm your understanding of their wants, preferences, and pain spots, do surveys, interviews, focus groups, or usability testing. This real-world feedback aids in the refinement of your product, marketing, and customer acquisition initiatives.

Monitor and Adapt:

Maintain a constant eye on the market, industry developments, and client behavior. Maintain flexibility and change your target client profiles as required. Market dynamics and client preferences might vary over time, so it's critical to remain on top of these shifts.

Conduct Surveys and Interviews:

Gather quantitative and qualitative data by engaging directly with potential consumers through surveys and interviews. Inquire about their requirements, pain spots, shopping history, and preferences. This personal knowledge can give significant insights and aid in the refinement of your target client profiles.

Use Analytics and Data:

Collect data about website traffic, social media participation, and consumer interactions using analytics tools and platforms. Analyze this information to learn about consumer habits, preferences, and conversion trends. These insights might help you identify your target customers and inform your marketing efforts.

Consider the Decision-Making Unit:

If your product or service includes B2B sales, understand the decision-making unit inside the businesses you are targeting. Determine the important decision-makers, influencers, and stakeholders in the purchase process. Customize your messaging and value proposition to meet their unique requirements and motivations.

Examine Psychographic elements:

Consider psychographic elements such as personality traits, values, interests, and lifestyles in addition to demographics. Understand how these characteristics impact the habits and preferences of your target clients. This greater understanding enables you to produce more focused marketing messages and stronger relationships with your target audience.

Identify Early Adopters:

Within your target market, look for early adopters who are more inclined to embrace innovation and explore new goods or services. Early adopters may give useful input, act as brand ambassadors, and help you establish market momentum. Determine their qualities and adapt your marketing to attract and engage them.

Examine the Customer Base of the Competitor:

Analyze your rivals' client base to acquire information into their target market. Identify overlaps and possible holes where your firm might offer a unique solution or better meet the demands of customers. Learn from your competitors' customer service achievements and failures.

Continuous Refinement and Testing:

As your business develops and changes, you should constantly revise and test your target consumer profiles. Seek client feedback, perform market research, and remain current on industry trends. Revisit and update your target client identification process on a regular basis to ensure it remains aligned with your company goals.

Create Buyer Personas:

Based on the insights and information you've obtained, create detailed buyer personas. These personas are imaginary individuals who represent various elements of your desired client base. Include information about their history, ambitions, difficulties, motivations, and preferred communication avenues. Make use of these personalities as a resource for your marketing and sales activities.

Remember that finding your target clients is a continuous process that necessitates a thorough grasp of their wants, habits, and preferences. You may successfully adjust your services and marketing messages to attract and keep your ideal clients by constantly refining your target customer profiles and modifying your strategy.

Developing a Value Proposition

Creating a solid value proposition for your business is critical because it articulates the distinct value you give to your target clients. A great value proposition distinguishes you from competition and connects with your target audience. Here's a step-by-step strategy to creating a strong value proposition:

Understand Your Target consumers:
Begin by learning all you can about your target consumers, including their wants, pain spots, objectives, and preferences. This comprehension serves as the foundation for developing a value offer that effectively meets their unique difficulties or aspirations.

Identify Customer Benefits:

Determine the major advantages that your product or service offers to your target customers. Consider the functional (what it accomplishes), emotional (how it makes clients feel), and social (how it impacts their image or standing). Concentrate on the outcomes or results that your consumers may expect if they use your solution.

Examine the Offerings of Competitors:

Examine your rivals' products and services, as well as their value propositions. Determine the holes or weaknesses in their services and how your business can deliver a distinct and greater value. This study will assist you in better positioning your value offer.

Define Your Differentiating Features:

Determine your startup's unique selling points (USPs)—the features that distinguish you from competition. Features, advantages, technology, quality, price, customer experience, and any other characteristic that gives a distinct edge might be included. Emphasize what makes your offering unique and appealing to your target audience.

Create a Simple and Effective Statement:

Summarize your value proposition in a brief sentence that illustrates the distinct value you offer. Keep it clear, understandable, and memorable. Focus on the major benefits or results that clients may expect from your solution and why they should select it over alternatives.

Share your value offer with your target clients and get feedback. Conduct surveys, interviews, or focus groups to learn about their reactions and whether or not they agree. Use this input to enhance and strengthen your value offer, ensuring that it properly speaks to your audience's requirements and preferences.

Differentiation:

Emphasize how your offering is distinct and superior than competitors in the market. Communicate the distinct qualities, perks, or experiences that distinguish you. Show why customers should select your startup over rivals, and how your value offer meets their unique pain points or goals.

Tailor for client groups:

If your firm serves numerous client groups, consider tailoring your value proposition to each segment's specific requirements and preferences. Adapt the messaging, advantages, or positioning to appeal to each target audience more powerfully.

Integrate into Communication Channels:

Incorporate your value proposition into all communication channels and consumer touchpoints. Make sure your website, marketing materials, social media accounts, and sales presentations are all consistent. At every engagement, your value offer should be clear, consistent, and obvious to potential consumers.

Continuously Evaluate and Adjust: Assess the success of your value offer on a regular basis as market dynamics and consumer demands change. Keep an eye on developments in the competition landscape and alter your value proposition as needed. Continuously get client feedback and assess how effectively your value offer is resonating with your target demographic.

Remember that your startup's message and positioning are built on a solid value proposition. It should clearly express the distinct value and benefits that you provide your consumers. You may differentiate your startup, attract clients, and get a significant competitive edge in the market by building a compelling value proposition.

Chapter 2: Crafting a Solid Business Plan

Outlining Your Business Model

Developing a strong business model is critical to the success of your startup. A business model describes how your organization develops, delivers, and collects value. Let's look at how to outline your business strategy in a fluid, continuous, and flowing fashion:

A well-crafted business model binds numerous aspects together effortlessly, providing a cohesive and integrated framework. It all starts with a clear grasp of your target consumers' wants, which will be the driving force behind your business. Knowing your consumers intimately allows you to tailor your value proposition to satisfy their needs in a unique and appealing way.

Consider the primary tasks that your startup must carry out in order to execute on that value offer. These tasks serve as the operational backbone of your company. Whether it's product development, manufacturing, service delivery, or a mix of the three, make sure it's all in line with your value proposition and consumer expectations.

Determine the resources needed to support these tasks at the same time. Intangible resources such as intellectual property, partnerships, or experienced individuals can be included as well as tangible resources such as equipment, technology, or facilities. Managing and exploiting these resources effectively improves your capacity to generate and provide value to consumers.

Consider the relationships you'll build with various stakeholders as you advance. Customers, suppliers, partners, and even rivals are all important components of your company ecosystem. Positive connections encourage cooperation, creativity, and sustainability. Consider how these interactions can help you to increase the value you create and capture.

Consider the income streams you'll produce in order to support your business strategy. Investigate various monetization options such as product sales, subscriptions, licensing, and advertising. Align your price with the perceived value you provide to your clients, providing a fair exchange that represents both their desire to pay and your need for profit.

Furthermore, consider the cost structure that drives your company strategy. Determine the primary cost drivers and strive for efficiency without sacrificing quality. To improve your cost structure, streamline processes, negotiate advantageous supplier contracts, and seek economies of scale.

Consider the methods via which you will contact your clients as you define your company concept. Consider the best distribution and marketing channels for increasing awareness, engaging customers, and facilitating product or service delivery. Based on your target market and industry conditions, use both online and offline channels, embracing digital transformation and conventional tactics.

Finally, as your firm changes, be adaptive and nimble. Review and improve your business model on a regular basis to ensure it stays relevant in the face of changing consumer wants, technology developments, and market trends. Accept failure, iterate on your ideas, and learn from both successes and failures.

Keep in mind that developing your business model is an iterative and flexible process. It necessitates a thorough understanding of your consumers, careful alignment of essential operations and resources, the development of strategic connections, and the creation of income streams while controlling expenses. Your company can traverse the complexity of the market, grasp opportunities, and prosper in a competitive marketplace if it has a well-crafted and constantly developing business model.

Setting Realistic Goals and Objectives

Setting realistic goals and objectives is a critical step in ensuring the success of your company. It entails setting specific and measurable goals to guide your activities and track your progress. Let us investigate this concept in a systematic and ongoing manner:

Setting achievable goals and objectives begins with imagining the future you want for your business. This vision acts as a guiding light, offering direction and meaning. It serves as a continuous thread connecting your current actions to the anticipated objectives.

Break down your vision into precise and quantifiable goals to make it a reality. Given your current resources, capabilities, and market circumstances, these objectives should be reachable within a reasonable timeframe. Align each objective with the mission and broader strategy of your business.

Next, define specific objectives that will function as stepping stones toward your ultimate aim. Objectives are defined, measurable goals that can be measured and tracked. They help you stay focused and track your progress along the road. Ensure that each aim is related to and helps to the attainment of your goals.

To keep your goals and objectives on track, evaluate and update them on a regular basis. Because of the changing nature of the business environment, course modifications or changes may be required. Regularly monitor your progress and make required adjustments to ensure your goals stay reasonable and in line with the development trajectory of your business.

When defining objectives, it is critical to use the SMART framework. Make sure your objectives are specific, measurable, attainable, relevant, and time-bound. This framework guarantees that your goals are well-defined, quantitative, attainable, connected with the aims of your business, and limited by a clear deadline.

Communicate your goals and objectives to your team, making certain that everyone is on the same page and knows their role in accomplishing them. Create a collaborative atmosphere that values feedback, input, and shared accountability. This promotes a sense of ownership and pushes your team to work together toward similar goals.

Celebrate milestones and accomplishments along the road to recognize progress and reinforce a culture of success. Track and monitor key performance indicators (KPIs) linked to your goals and objectives on a regular basis. This allows you to assess the success of your company, find areas for development, and make data-driven choices.

It is critical to strike a balance between establishing lofty objectives and being realistic. While pushing yourself and your team is important, establishing impossible objectives may lead to frustration and demotivation. Assess the viability of your goals on a regular basis, taking into account market dynamics, resource limits, and the stage of growth of your firm.

Setting realistic goals and objectives is critical to the success of your company. It entails setting specific and measurable goals to guide your activities and track your progress.

By imagining the future you want for your business, you create a continuous thread that ties your current actions to the outcomes you want. Break down your vision into concrete and quantifiable goals that can be achieved in a fair amount of time.

Set defined targets that function as stepping stones toward your goals to make your goals actionable. These goals are explicit, quantifiable, and related to the mission and strategy of your business. They give concentration and allow you to efficiently measure your development.

Review and alter your goals on a regular basis to keep up with the ever-changing business climate. This guarantees that your goals stay reasonable and in line with the trend of your startup's growth. To keep on track, evaluate your progress, modify your goals, and make any required course changes.

When developing objectives, keep the SMART framework in mind: Specific, Measurable, Achievable, Relevant, and Time-bound. This guarantees that your objectives are well-defined, quantified, achievable, and bound by clear timeframes.

Communicate your aims and objectives to your team, creating a collaborative environment that promotes shared accountability and ownership. Track key performance indicators (KPIs) relevant to your goals on a regular basis to assess the success of your startup, discover areas for development, and make educated decisions.

Strike a balance between establishing ambitious and realistic goals. Push yourself and your team, but avoid establishing unrealistic goals that might lead to demotivation. Assess the viability of your goals on a regular basis depending on market conditions, available resources, and the stage of growth of your firm.

Along the process, celebrate milestones and successes to recognize progress and reinforce a culture of success. This inspires your staff and fosters a happy and productive workplace atmosphere.

Setting realistic goals and objectives is critical to the success of your company. It entails setting specific and measurable goals to guide your activities and track your progress.

Begin by visualizing the future you want for your startup. This vision acts as a connecting link between your current actions and your intended objectives.

Divide your vision into precise, achievable targets. Given your existing resources and market circumstances, these objectives should be doable within a reasonable timeframe.

Establish defined objectives that serve as stepping stones toward your goals to make them actionable. These goals are explicit, quantifiable, and related to the mission and strategy of your business.

Review and alter your goals on a regular basis to keep up with the ever-changing business climate. This guarantees that your goals stay reasonable and in line with the trend of your startup's growth.

When developing objectives, keep the SMART framework in mind: Specific, Measurable, Achievable, Relevant, and Time-bound. This guarantees that your objectives are well-defined, quantified, achievable, aligned, and constrained by firm deadlines.

Communicate your team's aims and objectives, producing a collaborative environment that fosters shared accountability.

Track key performance indicators (KPIs) relating to your goals on a regular basis. This helps you to assess the success of your company, find areas for development, and make educated decisions.

Strike a balance between establishing ambitious and realistic goals. Assess the viability of your goals on a regular basis based on market circumstances and available resources.

Along the process, celebrate milestones and successes to recognize progress and reinforce a pleasant work atmosphere.

Setting attainable goals and objectives is a continuous process. Maintain focus on your vision, break it down into manageable tasks, define specific targets, and track progress on a regular basis. With a consistent and realistic strategy, you can propel your business to success and assure constant development toward your goals.

Creating a Financial Plan

Creating a financial plan is an important step in managing your startup's finances. It entails laying out your predicted revenues, costs, and cash flow in order to assure financial stability and assist decision-making. Let us investigate this concept in a systematic and ongoing manner:

Assessing your startup's financial goals and objectives is the first step in developing a financial strategy. Determine your financial goals, such as profitability, expansion, or financial sustainability.

Then, depending on your company strategy and market study, predict your income sources. Estimate your sales or revenue potential by taking into account aspects like price, market size, client acquisition rates, and expected demand. This lays the groundwork for understanding your revenue-generating potential.

Determine and estimate your startup's expenditures in each category. Consider operational, production, marketing, staff, overhead, and any other relevant expenditures. Make detailed and realistic estimates, accounting for both fixed and variable expenses.

Create a cash flow prediction by combining your anticipated revenues and expenses. This chart shows how money flows in and out of your business over time. It provides effective cash flow management by assisting you in identifying future financial shortfalls.

Analyze your financial data to determine your profitability, liquidity, and overall financial health. Key financial parameters such as gross margin, net profit margin, return on investment (ROI), and burn rate should be calculated. These ratios give information about your startup's financial performance and viability.

Consider many scenarios and do sensitivity analysis to determine the possible impact of market swings, pricing adjustments, or unforeseen costs. This helps you to predict probable problems and plan for them.

Create a budget that is in line with your financial objectives and expectations. Allocate resources to different parts of your organization, making sure that expenditure matches your strategic goals. Maintain financial discipline and optimize resource allocation by reviewing and adjusting your budget on a regular basis.

Include financial risk management methods in your strategy. Identify possible risks, such as market volatility, regulatory changes, or competitive pressures, and devise mitigation techniques to reduce their influence on your financial stability.

Seek expert counsel or talk with a financial professional to ensure that your financial strategy is accurate and successful. They may give useful insights, assist you in identifying blind spots, and ensuring your strategy is complete and feasible.

Monitor and measure your financial success versus your strategy on a regular basis. Examine your financial accounts, cash flow reports, and key performance indicators on a regular basis. This allows you to discover patterns, make educated judgments, and, if required, take remedial action in a timely manner.

Creating a financial strategy is critical for properly managing your startup's financial components. It entails laying out predicted revenues, costs, and cash flow in order to assure financial stability and guiding decision-making.

Begin by evaluating your financial goals and objectives. Determine your financial goals, whether they are for profitability, expansion, or sustainability.

Based on your company model and market data, forecast your revenue sources. Estimate sales or revenue potential by taking price, market size, client acquisition rates, and demand into account.

Determine and estimate your startup's expenditures in each category. Consider operating costs, manufacturing costs, marketing costs, employee wages, overhead, and other pertinent factors.

Create a cash flow forecast by combining predicted income and costs. This offers an overview of how money enters and exits your company. It aids in the identification of possible financial shortfalls and enables better cash flow management.

Assess profitability, liquidity, and overall financial health by analyzing financial data. Key financial parameters such as gross margin, net profit margin, ROI, and burn rate should be calculated. These ratios give information about the financial performance and viability of your company.

Consider several scenarios and do sensitivity analysis to better comprehend prospective market swings or expense adjustments. Prepare for problems by creating contingency plans.

Create a budget that is in line with your financial objectives and expectations. Allocate resources to different parts of your firm, making sure that expenditure corresponds to strategic goals. Review and revise the budget on a regular basis to optimize resource allocation.

Incorporate techniques for financial risk management. Determine possible threats, such as market volatility or regulatory changes. Create mitigating techniques to lessen the impact on financial stability.

Seek expert counsel or talk with a financial professional to ensure that your financial strategy is accurate and successful. They can give useful insights and aid in the identification of blind spots.

Monitor and assess financial performance versus the strategy on an ongoing basis. Examine financial statements, cash flow reports, and key performance indicators on a regular basis. This allows for the detection of patterns, informed decision-making, and prompt remedial action.

Making a financial plan is a continuous process. Maintain vigilance in monitoring and managing your money, update predictions on a regular basis, and change your strategy as your business grows. A well-structured and regularly evaluated financial plan serves as a road map for financial success, enabling long-term development and profitability.

Assessing Risks and Mitigation Strategies

Risk assessment and mitigation methods are critical components of managing uncertainties and guaranteeing the success of your company. It entails detecting possible risks, assessing their potential impact, and putting procedures in place to mitigate any negative outcomes. Let us investigate this concept in a systematic and ongoing manner:

Begin by thoroughly assessing all potential dangers to your startup. These risks might be internal or external, and they will differ depending on your industry, market conditions, or unique situations.

Assess the likelihood of occurrence and potential impact on your business for each highlighted risk. Consider the severity of the repercussions, the financial ramifications, operational interruptions, reputational harm, and any other relevant aspects to your startup.

Prioritize the risks based on their possible effect and likelihood, focusing on the most important ones. This helps you to direct resources and attention to places that demand it right now.

Create mitigation solutions for each risk that has been prioritized. Consider proactive strategies that can lower the possibility of risk occurrence or mitigate the effect of risk occurrence. Consider process improvements, redundancy plans, diversification, insurance, or partnerships as answers.

Implement the mitigating techniques identified by incorporating them into your operational procedures and decision-making frameworks. Check that the tactics are practical, achievable, and matched with the capabilities and resources of your business.

Monitor and evaluate the effectiveness of your mitigation techniques on a regular basis. Assess the evolving risk landscape, market dynamics, and emerging risks on a regular basis. Adapt your strategies as needed to manage new or emerging hazards.

Create a risk-awareness and risk-management culture within your startup. Encourage workers to identify and disclose possible hazards, establishing a collaborative and responsible risk management strategy.

Communicate and educate stakeholders on the identified risks and mitigation methods on a regular basis. This ensures that everyone understands their position and responsibilities in risk management.

Create a contingency plan to deal with unanticipated occurrences or hazards. This strategy describes the measures to be performed if a danger occurs, allowing for a quick and effective reaction.

Keep lines of communication open with essential stakeholders like as suppliers, partners, and customers. Collaborate closely with them to manage common risks and cooperatively handle any disruptions.

To reduce legal and compliance risks, monitor and comply with necessary legislation and legal requirements. Keep up to date on legislative developments that may affect your business operations and guarantee timely compliance.

As your business grows, review and update your risk assessment and mitigation measures on a regular basis. Conduct risk assessments on a regular basis to detect new hazards or changes in the risk environment.

You may reduce possible negative consequences on your company by regularly reviewing risks and executing effective mitigation techniques. A proactive and continuing approach to risk management assures your company's resilience and long-term success.

Building a Scalable Framework

Building a scalable foundation is critical for the growth and long-term success of your business. It entails developing a structure and processes capable of accommodating rising demand, growing operations, and changing market conditions.

Let us investigate this concept in a systematic and ongoing manner:

Begin by imagining your startup's development trajectory and long-term goals. Understand the scalability issues you may face as business grow and plan ahead of time to handle them.

Create a versatile organizational structure that allows for expansion and flexibility. Define the roles, responsibilities, and reporting lines that will allow for efficient decision-making and cooperation. Maintain open lines of communication and foster an agile and innovative culture.

Create scalable processes and systems capable of handling growing volume and complexity. Streamline operations, remove bottlenecks, and automate activities as much as feasible. As your startup expands, implement technology and solutions that promote efficiency and productivity.

Invest in scalable infrastructure, both physically and digitally. Plan for future demands and scalability in areas like as IT systems, manufacturing capacity, logistics, and customer service. To meet rising demand, use cloud computing, scalable hosting solutions, and scalable software platforms.

Develop a scalable culture in your startup. Encourage constant learning, flexibility, and an openness to change. Encourage a growth-oriented culture in which workers are encouraged to innovate, take responsibility, and contribute to scaling initiatives.

Scalability should be prioritized in the design of your product or service. Consider how readily your solution may be expanded, changed, or copied to meet the needs of a larger client base or new market sectors. Scalability should be built into your product plan and development methods.

Create scalable tactics for client acquisition and retention. Create scalable marketing strategies, take advantage of digital platforms, and improve client acquisition funnels. Implement customer relationship management (CRM) solutions to properly monitor and track customer interactions.

Track and assess scalability by monitoring key performance indicators (KPIs). Metrics such as revenue growth, client acquisition rate, customer retention rate, conversion rates, and operational efficiency should all be measured. Analyze data on a regular basis to find areas for improvement and to maximize scaling efforts.

Form strategic alliances and collaborations to capitalize on common resources and skills. Identify synergistic possibilities and develop strategic relationships to advance your scaling objectives.

As your startup grows, evaluate and adapt your scalable foundation on a regular basis. Review your strategy, procedures, and systems on a regular basis to verify they are still in line with company growth goals. Maintain your flexibility and responsiveness to market changes, client input, and developing prospects.

You position your business for long-term development and adaptation by creating a scalable architecture. It enables you to satisfy rising demand, enter new markets, and capitalize on growing possibilities. Scalability should be embraced as a basic idea and integrated into all elements of your startup's operations to ensure long-term success.

Chapter 3: Building an Effective Team

Defining Roles and Responsibilities

Defining roles and duties inside your business is critical for fostering clarity, responsibility, and successful teamwork. It entails describing the particular responsibilities and expectations for each role in your firm. Let us investigate this concept in a systematic and ongoing manner:

Begin by doing a comprehensive examination of your startup's requirements and goals. Determine the essential responsibilities and areas that need specialist roles in order to support your business operations and accomplish your objectives.

Create a robust organizational structure for your business that describes the hierarchy and reporting lines. Define the critical roles and positions required to carry out the different duties and responsibilities.

Define the particular responsibilities and activities associated with each job. Outline both the primary responsibilities and any additional expectations or needs. This clarity ensures that employees understand their area of work and can properly carry out their tasks.

Consider the relevant abilities, credentials, and experience for each post. Define the required abilities and characteristics for employees to flourish in their roles. This aids you in the recruiting and selection process by ensuring that candidates are a suitable fit for their assigned responsibilities.

Assign positions depending on individuals' talents, competencies, and interests inside your business. Utilize your team members' unique abilities to increase productivity and work happiness.

Encourage collaboration and synergy across roles by outlining interdependencies and areas of shared responsibility. Clarify how various positions should collaborate to ensure smooth coordination and successful cooperation.

Create distinct reporting lines to provide a clear flow of information and decision-making processes. Define who each job reports to and how your startup's communication channels should work.

As your business grows, evaluate and update position descriptions on a regular basis. Maintain flexibility and responsiveness to changes in company requirements, market dynamics, and growth prospects. Adapt roles and duties to reflect changing needs and guarantee alignment with the strategic direction of your business.

Effectively communicate job objectives and obligations to your team members. Individuals should have a thorough grasp of their positions, including their purpose, goals, and performance standards. Create an atmosphere that invites free debate and explanations.

Encourage employees to take responsibility for their allocated responsibilities and contribute to the overall success of your business by encouraging autonomy and ownership within each function.

Assess and evaluate people' performance in their particular responsibilities on a regular basis. Give comments, encourage professional development, and celebrate accomplishments. Proactively address any performance gaps or issues to ensure continual progress.

By explicitly outlining roles and duties, you provide the groundwork for effective cooperation, responsibility, and productivity inside your business. This clarity guarantees that everyone understands their duties and how they contribute to the organization's overall success. It fosters a healthy work atmosphere and allows workers to focus on their areas of expertise, propelling your business forward.

Recruiting Top Talent

Recruiting great people is critical to your startup's success and development. It entails attracting and choosing highly trained and qualified personnel who can contribute to the aims and culture of your firm. Let us investigate this concept in a systematic and ongoing manner:

Establish Your Ideal Candidate:

Clearly define the skills, experience, and credentials necessary for the position for which you are recruiting. Outline the important talents and traits that correspond with the values and goals of your company. This will direct your search and choices.

Create an Engaging Employer Brand:

Create a compelling employer brand that highlights your startup's unique culture, mission, and growth potential. Highlight the value proposition you provide to potential workers and set yourself out from competition. To raise awareness and recruit top personnel, use digital channels, social media, and employer review sites.

Create Eye-Catching Job Descriptions:

Create job descriptions that are clear, succinct, and intriguing. Highlight the interesting parts of the position and the ambition of your business. Highlight the opportunity for development, learning, and influence. To attract diverse talent, use inclusive language in your descriptions and make sure they resonate with your intended audience.

Use a range of Recruitment Channels:

Use a range of recruitment channels to reach a diverse group of prospects. Online job boards, professional networking sites, social media platforms, industry-specific forums, and referrals from your current network are all possibilities. To broaden your reach, consider working with recruiting firms or visiting job fairs.

Develop an organized and Thorough Selection Process:

Create an organized and thorough selection process that involves various phases such as resume screening, interviews, skills tests, and reference checks. Ensure that each phase is structured to analyze candidates' fit with your startup's culture and values against stated criteria.

Conduct Competency-based Interviews:

During interviews, ask behavioral and situational questions to assess candidates' skills, experience, and problem-solving abilities. To elicit concrete instances of their prior successes and how they connect with the needs of the position, use the STAR (Situation, Task, Action, Result) technique.

Assess Cultural Fit:

During the selection process, pay close attention to cultural fit. Examine if applicants share your company's values, working style, and team dynamics. Consider doing informal meetings or team-building exercises to determine their fit with your current team members.

Provide Competitive Compensation and Benefits:

Research and benchmark industry compensation and benefit standards to ensure your offer is competitive. To recruit top personnel, consider extra incentives such as stock options, flexible work arrangements, professional development opportunities, and a good work atmosphere.

Provide a Positive Candidate Experience:

Ensure that candidates have a positive and efficient experience throughout the recruiting process. Keep candidates aware of progress and future actions by communicating clearly, immediately, and honestly. Maintain a favorable reputation by providing comments to all candidates, even those who are not chosen.

Develop a robust onboarding approach to assist new hires in integrating successfully into your business. Give them the training, resources, and support they need to be productive and successful in their positions. To retain and engage great personnel, provide a friendly and inclusive atmosphere.

Remember that finding great talent is a constant process. Refine your recruitment strategies on a regular basis depending on feedback and market developments. To recruit and retain the top candidates, cultivate a strong employer brand and reputation. You can establish a competent team that drives the success of your business by spending time and effort in the recruitment process.

Fostering a Culture of Collaboration

Fostering a collaborative culture is critical for establishing a cohesive and effective work environment inside your business. It entails creating an environment in which people can work together, exchange ideas, and collaborate toward common goals. Let us investigate this concept in a systematic and ongoing manner:

Lead by Example:

As a leader, model collaborative behaviors and participate actively in collaborative endeavors. Encourage open communication, cooperation, and an openness to listening to and learning from others. The tone of the team is set by your activities.

Create a Shared Vision and Goals:

Communicate your startup's vision and long-term ambitions to the whole staff. Ensure that everyone knows how their particular efforts relate to the larger goals. This shared understanding promotes a feeling of common purpose and encourages teamwork.

Make Collaboration Opportunities:

Create routines and processes that promote cooperation. Encourage cross-functional collaboration by developing communication and cooperation channels between various teams or departments. To enable knowledge sharing and collaborative problem-solving, use project management tools or collaborative platforms.

Encourage Open Communication:

Create a climate in which people feel free to communicate their ideas, concerns, and comments. Encourage active listening and respect for other points of view. To build a collaborative culture, emphasize the need of productive and courteous communication.

Encourage Interdisciplinary Collaboration:

Encourage personnel with diverse backgrounds, expertise, and experiences to work on projects or initiatives together. Create an atmosphere that honors different points of view and supports interdisciplinary learning. Cross-pollination of ideas can result in novel solutions.

Recognize and Reward Collaborative contributions:

Recognize and reward collaborative contributions inside your startup. Celebrate successful cooperation and honor people or teams that work well together. Implement prizes or incentives to foster collaboration and collaborative behaviour.

Create Physical or Virtual Collaborative locations: Establish physical or virtual locations that promote cooperation, such as open work areas or digital collaboration platforms. These environments promote chance encounters, information exchange, and idea development. Shared spaces can help to foster a sense of belonging and cooperation.

Foster Trust and Psychological Safety: Create an atmosphere in which people feel secure taking chances, sharing their thoughts, and challenging the status quo. Encourage a trusting atmosphere in which errors are viewed as learning opportunities and various viewpoints are respected. Open cooperation and invention are encouraged by psychological safety.

Support Training and Skill Development: Give staff opportunity to improve their cooperation abilities. Provide workshops or training programs on effective communication, conflict resolution, and teamwork. Individuals will be able to interact more successfully as a result of this investment in skill development.

Evaluate and Adjust: Constantly assess the efficacy of your combined efforts. Seek input from workers and track collaborative outcomes. Adjust tactics and activities in response to feedback and changing demands to constantly enhance your collaborative culture.

By building a collaborative culture, you create an atmosphere in which teamwork, creativity, and collective success thrive. Collaboration improves problem-solving, decision-making, and creative thinking inside your company, resulting in higher productivity and a better sense of togetherness among team members.

Establishing Leadership and Communication Channels

Establishing good leadership and communication channels inside your business is critical for encouraging clarity, alignment, and fruitful cooperation. It entails putting in place structures and processes that allow for clear guidance, open communication, and efficient decision-making.

Begin by establishing your startup's leadership positions and duties. Determine who will lead and steer the team in reaching organizational goals. Create a structure that allows for effective decision-making and accountability.

Communicate the vision, purpose, and goals of your business to the whole team. Ensure that everyone knows the general goals and how their individual contributions contribute to the overall success. This collaboration promotes a common sense of purpose and direction.

Transparency is demonstrated through freely sharing information, updates, and choices with the team. Be receptive to input, foster debate, and respond to issues as soon as possible.

Transparent leadership fosters trust and encourages collaboration.

Establish consistent communication routes to keep the team informed and connected. Team meetings, newsletters, or digital platforms for disseminating updates, progress reports, and key announcements are examples of this. Consistent communication promotes a sense of belonging and encourages participation.

Encourage two-way communication so that team members may share their thoughts, concerns, and suggestions. Create an atmosphere that encourages active listening and polite discourse. Accept different points of view and tap into your team's collective wisdom.

Allow for face-to-face contacts by holding frequent team meetings, casual gatherings, or team-building activities. In-person communication develops team relationships, fosters trust, and fosters a sense of camaraderie.

Use digital communication technologies to make information exchange more fluid and efficient. Use chat platforms, project management software, and video conferencing to allow for real-time communication regardless of where team members are located.

Encourage an open feedback and constructive criticism culture. Encourage frequent performance reviews in which employees get direction, acknowledgment for their accomplishments, and suggestions for development. Effective feedback enhances connections and promotes individual and team development.

Give leaders and managers the tools they need to communicate successfully with their staff. Give them the skills and resources they need to communicate clearly and effectively. Help them to motivate and inspire their team members.

Evaluate the efficacy of your communication channels and leadership strategies on a regular basis. Seek input from team members, review results, and make necessary improvements. Improve your communication methods on a regular basis to keep up with new demands and technology.

By building efficient leadership and communication channels, you can foster an atmosphere in which ideas flow, collaboration thrives, and teams work together to achieve common goals. This builds a culture of trust, involvement, and creativity, allowing your business to effectively handle hurdles and capture opportunities.

Nurturing Employee Motivation and Engagement

Employee engagement and motivation are critical for developing a good and effective work environment inside your firm. It entails cultivating a culture that appreciates and supports employees, giving chances for advancement, and cultivating a feeling of purpose and fulfillment. Let's take a slow and easy approach to this concept:

Begin by knowing your workers' particular needs and objectives. Recognize that each individual is unique and that different reasons may inspire them. Spend time listening, communicating, and developing connections with your team members.

Make your workplace a welcoming and inclusive place where employees feel valued and appreciated. Recognize and recognize their efforts and accomplishments. Encourage a sense of belonging by providing chances for cooperation and teamwork.

Provide each staff with clear objectives and goals. Establish quantifiable goals that are in line with their jobs and the broader goals of the business. This clarity assists employees in understanding how their job contributes to the larger picture.

Provide possibilities for advancement and development. Provide workers with training programs, workshops, and mentorship opportunities to assist them improve their skills and expertise. Encourage them to take on new tasks and responsibilities that correspond to their interests and professional objectives.

Encourage appropriate limits and flexibility whenever feasible to promote work-life balance. Recognize the value of personal well-being and assist employees in creating a harmonic balance between work and personal life.

Encourage open dialogue and feedback. Establish outlets for employees to share their thoughts, concerns, and suggestions. Create a culture that recognizes and respects different points of view, fostering a sense of ownership and empowerment among team members.

Recognize and appreciate employee accomplishments and efforts. Implement a fair and transparent recognition program that goes beyond monetary awards to recognize great effort.

This might involve public recognition, prospects for advancement, or new duties.

Encourage autonomy and ownership by giving workers the resources, power, and trust they need to make decisions and take responsibility of their work. Allow them to develop, explore, and contribute to the startup's growth and success.

Check in with employees on a regular basis to measure their contentment, engagement, and motivation. Conduct frequent performance reviews to offer feedback, resolve issues, and help them grow professionally. Demonstrate genuine concern for their well-being and professional goals.

As a helpful and motivated leader, set a good example. Exhibit zeal, desire, and a positive attitude. Inspire and encourage your staff by demonstrating your passion to the startup's goals and principles.

Evaluate and enhance staff motivation and engagement tactics on a regular basis. Seek input from workers, evaluate data, and remain up to date on industry best practices. Adapt your tactics to match your team members' changing requirements and expectations.

You can create an atmosphere where employees feel appreciated, empowered, and inspired to give their all by cultivating employee motivation and engagement. This results in enhanced productivity, job happiness, and, ultimately, the success of your business.

Chapter 4: Funding Your Startup

Self-Funding and Bootstrapping

Self-funding and bootstrapping are methods of financing your business without relying on other sources of capital. They entail employing your own resources and creating income internally to support the operations and growth of your organization. Let's take a slow and easy approach to this concept:

Self-funding your firm entails leveraging personal funds, investments, or assets to finance it. It enables you to retain total control and ownership of your company without diluting equity or incurring debt. You may establish and run your company on your own terms by using your own resources.

The practice of operating and expanding a business with low financial means is referred to as bootstrapping. It necessitates meticulous financial management, with a focus on earning income from early consumers or clients in order to sustain ongoing operations and expansion. Bootstrapping promotes a lean and cost-effective company model.

Begin with examining your own financial condition in order to self-fund and bootstrap your business. Determine how much cash you can put into your firm without endangering your own finances. Personal savings, retirement assets, or investments may be included.

Create a comprehensive financial strategy including your startup's estimated costs, income streams, and cash flow. Prioritize key costs and look for methods to reduce overhead and wasteful spending. Find cost-effective solutions for your company demands by being inventive and innovative.

Priority should be given to earning early income by gaining paying consumers or clients. Market your product or service to target buyers by providing a compelling value proposition. Prioritize sales and marketing activities to increase income.

Manage your cash flow carefully to ensure you have enough finances to meet operating expenditures. To increase cash flow, regularly monitor spending, negotiate advantageous terms with suppliers, and be proactive in handling accounts receivable.

Consider other strategies of financing expansion, such as reinvesting revenues or finding strategic alliances. Look for ways to partner with other firms or to use existing networks to gain access to resources and possibilities.

Maintain a lean and agile attitude in the early phases of your business, and be prepared to make required sacrifices and trade-offs. To save expenses and enhance efficiency, be prepared to wear numerous hats and take on diverse jobs.

Keep your money management habits focused and diligent. Evaluate and alter your strategy on a regular basis based on the performance of your startup and market conditions. Prioritize investments that provide the best return on investment and are in line with your growth goals.

By self-funding and bootstrapping, you retain control over the fate of your firm while still laying a solid financial basis. Discipline, resourcefulness, and perseverance are required. While slower growth may be required at first, it may provide you with a solid financial foundation and position your firm for long-term sustainability and success.

Seeking Angel Investors and Venture Capitalists

Seeking angel investors and venture capitalists is a technique for obtaining outside investment for your firm. These investors contribute funds in return for stock or a stake in your company. Let's take a slow and easy approach to this concept:

Individuals who spend their own money in early-stage enterprises are known as angel investors. They frequently have previous entrepreneurial experience and are ready to take on more risks. Angel investors often contribute initial capital to assist firms in getting off to a good start. They provide coaching, industry contacts, and experience in addition to cash assistance.

Professional investors who handle funds from diverse sources, such as institutional investors and high-net-worth individuals, are known as venture capitalists (VCs). Venture capitalists often invest in firms that have shown commercial potential and scalability. They give larger investment rounds later in the startup's development. VCs frequently play an active role in the management and strategic direction of the firms in which they invest.

Begin by perfecting your company strategy and pitch before approaching angel investors and venture capitalists. Explain your startup's value proposition, market potential, and growth plan in detail. Present an engaging tale that piques the curiosity of the investors and illustrates how their investment will yield profits.

Investigate and find angel investor networks, angel groups, or venture capital firms that are relevant to your sector and stage of development. To meet possible investors, attend networking events, pitch competitions, or conferences. Make use of internet platforms and directories that allow the introduction of entrepreneurs and investors.

Prepare a detailed investor presentation deck that shows critical KPIs, financial projections, competitive advantage, and team expertise for your business. Tailor your proposal to each investor's or firm's individual interests and investment requirements.

Establish contact with possible investors. Seek warm introductions through your network or contacts in your field. Personal relationships and referrals may boost your credibility and raise your chances of obtaining funding. Throughout the process, maintain professional and honest communication.

Prepare for investor due diligence. Expect comprehensive financials, market research, customer validation, and legal paperwork needs. Set up a data room or virtual data room to safely communicate sensitive information.

Negotiate the terms and structure of the investment. Be informed of the investment's worth, ownership interest, governance rights, and any other requirements. Seek legal and financial counsel to ensure that you fully comprehend the ramifications of the investment agreement.

Once you have secured financing, use the funds carefully to carry out your company strategy and reach your development objectives. Maintain frequent contact and updates with your investors, keeping them up to date on your startup's growth. Use their experience and network to help you expand faster.

It is critical to understand that soliciting external investment from angel investors or venture capitalists is a selective and competitive process. Not all firms are candidates for this sort of finance, and it is critical to thoroughly consider the conditions and ramifications of taking investment. Ascertain that your startup's vision, goals, and long-term strategies are in sync.

By approaching angel investors and venture capitalists, you can have access to funding, knowledge, and networks that can help your firm thrive. However, it is critical to approach this process carefully, extensively investigate possible investors, and ensure that the investment corresponds with the vision and objectives of your firm.

Crowdfunding and Alternative Financing Options

Crowdfunding and other alternative financing sources might help your firm get funds. These methods entail enlisting a huge number of people or organizations to donate cash in exchange for prizes, equity, or loans. Let's take a slow and easy approach to this concept:

Crowdfunding systems allow entrepreneurs to raise financing from a broad group of people known as backers or supporters. Startups establish crowdfunding campaigns to convey their business ideas, ambitions, and financing requirements. Backers can give monies at various levels in exchange for prizes or perks.

Reward-based crowdfunding is providing rewards to supporters who donate cash to your campaign, such as early access to items, unique experiences, or personalized stuff. It enables you to raise donations while also developing a network of fans who are enthusiastic about your product or concept.

You may sell shares or ownership in your business to a group of investors through equity-based crowdfunding. Backers become shareholders and have a financial stake in your company's success. This strategy may appeal to investors looking for a potential return on their investment.

Debt-based crowdfunding, commonly referred to as peer-to-peer lending, is borrowing money from people or organizations using online platforms. Startups are provided with loans that have preset interest rates and repayment terms. This option allows you to obtain financing while keeping management and ownership of your company.

Alternative fundraising possibilities, in addition to crowdfunding, include:

Business incubators and accelerators: These programs provide entrepreneurs assistance, coaching, and frequently early money in exchange for equity or involvement in their growth.

Grants and government funding: Startups may be eligible for research grants, small company awards, or industry-specific grants. Investigate any government-sponsored initiatives that provide financial assistance or incentives for innovation and entrepreneurship.

Collaborations and sponsorships with established corporations or organizations interested in aiding startups in your field. Seek collaborations or sponsorships that will give financial resources or access to networks and resources.

Financing from a supplier or a customer: Negotiate longer payment terms with suppliers or look into prepayment alternatives with customers. This can assist improve your cash flow and give possibilities for short-term funding.

Bootstrapping: Fund your firm with personal savings, credit cards, or loans from friends and family. This method allows you to retain control and ownership while requiring careful financial management and risk evaluation.

When exploring crowdfunding or alternative financing methods, conduct thorough research and select the technique that best fits your business model, growth goals, and finance requirements. To increase your chances of success, develop a great pitch, have a strong web presence, and utilize your networks.

When dealing with supporters, lenders, or investors, keep in mind that trust and openness are essential. Communicate your company idea, progress, and risks connected with the investment in a clear and concise manner. Keep your supporters informed and engaged on a regular basis to develop a feeling of community and accountability.

By investigating crowdsourcing and alternative financing methods, you may acquire funds while harnessing the support and excitement of your backers or partners. These tactics can give the financial resources required to propel your startup's growth while also increasing your network and confirming your company concept.

Pitching to Potential Investors

Pitching potential investors is an important stage in obtaining money for your firm. It entails persuasively and concisely presenting your business idea, value proposition, market potential, and financial predictions to potential investors. Let's take a slow and easy approach to this concept:

Understand your target audience:
Investigate and comprehend the background, interests, and investment preferences of the possible investors to whom you will pitch. Customize your proposal to meet their investment requirements and demonstrate how your business meets their investment thesis.

Create an engaging story:
Create an engaging story that communicates the problem your firm addresses, the market opportunity, and your unique value offer. Highlight the pain issues that your target audience is experiencing and how your solution successfully solves those pain points.

Keep it focused and concise: Keep your pitch focused and concise. Aim to communicate your main point in a couple minutes or less. Prepare an elevator pitch that successfully conveys the core of your business and attracts investors' attention.

Emphasize the market opportunity:

Clearly explain your target market's size, growth potential, and dynamics. Demonstrate your knowledge of market trends, client demands, and the competitive environment. Show how your startup is unique and offers a compelling market advantage.

Showcase your group:

Introduce your team and their relevant skills, emphasizing their accomplishments and credentials. Investors want to see a skilled and unified workforce that can effectively execute the company plan.

Describe your company model:

Explain how your firm makes income, your pricing plan, and your business model's scalability. Showcase your customer acquisition, retention, and monetization strategies. Customer testimonials or pilot project outcomes might be used to demonstrate traction or early validation.

Financial predictions:

Present realistic and well-supported financial estimates that indicate your startup's development potential. Highlight important financial data such as sales projections, gross margins, and predicted profitability. Explain the data' assumptions and growth factors.

Address risk management and mitigation strategies:

Recognize the risks and obstacles that your startup may encounter, as well as ways for managing those risks. Demonstrate that you have a realistic grasp of market dynamics and that you have examined potential roadblocks. Investors like entrepreneurs that are proactive and have backup plans in place.

Show traction and milestones:

Share any major collaborations, customer acquisition, product development progress, or revenue growth that you have accomplished. Highlight any industry experts' or significant publications' acknowledgement or validation.

Be enthusiastic and confident:

Display excitement and confidence in your pitch. Investors not only invest in ideas, but also in the entrepreneurs who put them into action. Show your enthusiasm for your company and your commitment to succeed.

Be prepared to answer the following questions:

Anticipate potential investors' inquiries and be prepared to respond thoughtfully and concisely. Practice your pitch in front of others to improve your delivery and address any gaps or weak spots.

Remember that your pitch's purpose is to pique the curiosity of potential investors and gain follow-up meetings or conversations. Continuously tweak and customize your pitch in response to feedback and lessons learned from each contact. Maintain your resilience and persistence, as obtaining finance sometimes takes several pitches and interactions with various investors.

Negotiating and Structuring Deals

Deal negotiation and structuring is a dynamic process that entails establishing common ground and formalizing agreements amongst the parties involved. Effective communication, adaptability, and the ability to navigate difficult issues are required.

To begin, it is critical to create a good and constructive bargaining environment. Encourage open dialogue, active listening, and respect for all parties' opinions and interests. Building trust and rapport lays the groundwork for a fruitful negotiation process.

Thorough planning is essential. Investigate the other party's background, goals, and prior transactions to better grasp their motives and preferences. Gather market data, industry trends, and benchmarks to back up your negotiating positions and arguments.

Define your goals and priorities clearly, recognizing where you are prepared to compromise and where you will not. This clarity allows you to concentrate throughout talks and make sound conclusions.

Actively listen to the opposing party's points of view and concerns during the discussion. Investigate their fundamental interests and objectives. Look for points of agreement and chances for mutually beneficial results.

Present your plans and arguments with passion and clarity, backed up with evidence and persuasive logic. Prepare to respond to objections and counteroffers by proposing alternate solutions or concessions that still match with your goals.

Negotiation frequently includes give and take. Be open to make concessions and be flexible, but also know your limitations and be prepared to walk away if the transaction does not line with the best interests of your business. Seek a win-win situation that benefits both sides.

As you achieve an agreement on crucial elements, it's critical to document and formalize the transaction using legally enforceable contracts or agreements. Consider retaining legal advice to ensure that the terms are correctly constructed and that all parties' rights and interests are protected.

Maintain open and transparent communication throughout the negotiating and transaction structuring process. Address any issues or misconceptions as soon as possible to avoid future problems. To develop a long-term connection with the other party, cultivate a sense of collaboration and goodwill.

Remember that negotiating is about more than simply obtaining an agreement; it is also about developing connections and laying the groundwork for future partnerships. Maintain continued contact and create a favorable connection even after the contract is formed to maximize the possible benefits of the agreement.

You may negotiate advantageous terms, develop strategic relationships, and position your business for growth and success by mastering the art of negotiating and structuring transactions. Adopt a flexible and collaborative approach, be open to new opportunities, and strive for mutually beneficial outcomes.

Chapter 5: Product Development and Launch

Conducting Prototyping and Iterative Design

Iterative design and prototyping are dynamic and creative processes that drive product development. It entails developing early versions of your product, soliciting input, and constantly refining and enhancing its design.

To begin, think and explore several ideas to produce basic notions. Consider the problem you want to address, the demands of your users, and market trends. This creative phase allows you to brainstorm and imagine many options for your product.

Create prototypes to bring your ideas to life. Depending on the nature of your product, prototypes might range from simple sketches and wireframes to interactive mockups or real models. The idea is to build physical representations of your design that can be tested and evaluated.

Share your prototypes with target users, stakeholders, and industry experts. Encourage them to provide their thoughts on usability, functionality, and overall experience. This input is essential in identifying areas for improvement and validating design assumptions.

Iterate on your design based on the input you've received, making any required changes and improvements. This iterative process include fine-tuning your prototypes, fixing usability concerns, and incorporating feedback to build a more polished and user-centered design.

Repeat this cycle of prototype, feedback, and iteration several times. Each iteration gets you one step closer to a final design that satisfies user demands, addresses pain spots, and is consistent with your product vision. Accept comments and accept the potential for growth with an open mind.

Consider performing user testing and usability studies as you proceed through iterations to obtain a better understanding of how your target consumers interact with your product. This user-centered approach assists you in identifying usability issues and making informed design decisions.

Maintain good communication and cooperation among your team throughout the prototype and iterative design phase. Encourage interdisciplinary cooperation, in which designers, engineers, and other stakeholders collaborate to improve the product design.

During the prototype and design phases, embrace agility and adaptability. Be open to pivot and investigate alternate options if feedback shows that modifications are required. To swiftly evaluate concepts and iterate on changes, prioritize speed and efficiency in your prototyping process.

Prototyping and iterative design guarantee that your product grows in response to customer input and market demands. This method decreases the risk of creating a product that does not fulfill the demands of the consumer or falls short of expectations. Accept the process's creative and iterative character, and commit to refining and developing your design until you reach an ideal solution.

Testing and Validating Your Product

A critical phase in the product development process is testing and verifying your product. It entails doing thorough assessments and receiving feedback to ensure that your product fits user demands, operates well, and adds value. Let's take a slow and easy approach to this concept:

Begin by outlining the goals of your product testing. Define the precise elements you wish to assess, such as usability, functionality, performance, or dependability. This clarity will drive the testing process and guarantee that meaningful insights are gathered.

Create test scenarios that represent real-world circumstances and user interactions with your product. Take into account various user personas, use circumstances, and potential edge cases. Make a systematic testing strategy that covers all areas of your product and specifies the testing approaches you will use.

Follow the given test cases to carry out your testing plan. Depending on the nature of your product and the available resources, use a combination of human and automated testing methodologies. Any issues or defects discovered during testing should be documented and tracked for remediation.

Collect feedback from target users or a representative sample of your target market. To learn more about your customers' experiences with your product, do user interviews, surveys, or usability testing. Seek both qualitative and quantitative feedback to learn about use, satisfaction, and potential areas for development.

Analyze the information and feedback gathered during testing. Identify patterns, trends, and user-reported pain points. Prioritize the concerns based on their influence on the user experience and fix them in future product revisions.

Iterate and enhance your product depending on customer feedback and insights gathered from testing. Based on the discovered faults and recommendations, incorporate the necessary modifications, modify the user interface, and optimize performance. Continuously tweak and iterate your product until it meets or surpasses user expectations.

Consider beta testing or pilot projects with a small sample of users or clients. This gives you the ability to collect real-world usage statistics and evaluate your product in a controlled setting. During this phase, keep an eye on user input, behavior, and satisfaction and make any required changes before the official product launch.

Check that your testing and validation procedures are in accordance with industry standards, laws, and compliance needs. Follow data protection and privacy policies, accessibility requirements, and any other applicable legal or ethical issues.

Keep in mind that testing and verifying your product is a continuous process. Continue to test your product as it changes and new features are added to guarantee its performance, usability, and effectiveness. To maintain your product competitive and user-centric, get customer input on a regular basis, watch market trends, and stay tuned in to changing user demands.

You boost your chances of producing a high-quality, user-focused solution by extensively testing and verifying your product. It enables you to discover and solve any problems or flaws early on, resulting in a more successful and well-received product on the market.

Incorporating Customer Feedback

Customer feedback is an essential technique in product development and business success. It entails actively soliciting and listening to consumer feedback, interpreting their insights, and implementing changes based on their comments.

To begin, provide many avenues for clients to submit feedback. Surveys, feedback forms, social media interactions, customer service channels, and specific feedback sessions are examples of these. Make it simple for clients to express themselves and encourage them to do so.

Pay close attention to what your consumers are saying and actively listen to their opinions. Analyze the input to determine trends, frequent problems, and areas for improvement. Positive and negative feedback should both be examined since they give vital insights into what is functioning effectively and what needs to be improved.

Prioritize and categorize customer input based on its impact on the user experience, frequency of occurrence, and alignment with the vision and goals of your product. Concentrate on the input that has the most potential to improve customer happiness and meet their requirements.

Maintain open and honest contact with your consumers. Recognize and appreciate their input, and assure them that their opinions have been heard. Provide regular updates on how their suggestions are being evaluated and implemented.

Collaborate across departments within your firm to assess the feasibility and effect of incorporating client input. Product managers, designers, developers, and other relevant stakeholders should be included in the decision-making process. Evaluate the proposed modifications' technical feasibility, resource needs, and potential consequences as a group.

Changes should be implemented depending on the insights gathered from client input. Prioritize upgrades that are in line with your product plan and will have the most beneficial influence on the user experience. Communicate these modifications to your clients, emphasizing how their feedback has aided in the enhancements.

Monitor and analyze the impact of executed modifications on a continuous basis. Seek continuous feedback from clients to assess their happiness and gain further insights. This iterative feedback loop guarantees that your product is constantly refined depending on client demands and preferences.

Incorporating consumer input is a continuous process that shows your dedication to providing a customer-centric service. You can strengthen your customer connections, improve product quality, and generate customer loyalty and advocacy by actively listening, assessing, and making changes based on their feedback.

Remember that the customer's voice is a crucial asset in molding the success of your product. Adopt a customer-centric culture, solicit feedback on a regular basis, and use it as a compass to steer your product development and commercial choices.

Planning a Successful Product Launch

A successful product launch requires careful planning in order to introduce your product to the market and generate enthusiasm among your target audience. It entails creating a thorough strategy, organizing numerous operations, and carrying out a well-executed launch plan.

Begin by defining specific goals for your product launch. Define your goals, whether they be to increase revenue, raise brand recognition, get new consumers, or all of the above. These goals will guide your strategy and help you assess the effectiveness of your launch.

Understand your target audience from head to toe. Conduct market research, collect consumer feedback, and develop buyer personas to understand their wants, preferences, and problem areas. This information will help you customize your messaging, positioning, and communication channels to resonate with your target demographic.

Create a detailed launch strategy that specifies essential features and actions. Define your unique selling proposition, market positioning, and target market segments. Determine the most successful marketing channels and approaches for reaching your target demographic, taking into account a combination of digital and conventional means.

Create an engaging brand narrative and language that shows your product's features and value. Create original and compelling material that piques the curiosity and attention of your target audience. Align your messaging with your brand's identity and your customers' aspirations.

Coordinate your marketing and communication activities in the run-up to the launch to develop anticipation and momentum. To build buzz and raise awareness, use a combination of online and offline channels such as social media, email marketing, press releases, influencer collaborations, and events.

Consider providing unique pre-launch previews, early access, or incentives to generate excitement and early adopters. Increase your reach and generate word-of-mouth referrals by using your existing client base, influencers, and industry contacts.

Make sure your product is completely ready for launch by thoroughly testing and improving it. To produce a high-quality product that surpasses client expectations, address any bugs, usability difficulties, or performance concerns.

Prepare your sales and customer service teams to manage enquiries and provide help both before and after the launch. Train them on the features, advantages, and commonly asked questions about the product. Provide the tools and resources required to properly handle client demands.

Keep a tight eye on the launch, measure critical data, and solicit consumer feedback. Evaluate the success of your launch efforts on a regular basis and make changes as needed. Analyze the data to learn about consumer behavior, market reaction, and opportunities for development.

Follow up with post-launch marketing campaigns to maintain momentum and engage your audience even more. To cultivate long-term connections with customers, implement customer retention methods like as loyalty programs or tailored communication.

Evaluate the success of your product launch against your established goals on a regular basis. Sales, client acquisition, internet traffic, social media engagement, and customer feedback are all key performance indicators (KPIs). Use the experience to improve future product launches.

You may develop a strong market presence, generate enthusiasm, and optimize the success of your product in the marketplace by preparing and executing a well-thought-out product launch strategy. You can set the groundwork for a successful launch and continuous business growth with careful planning, excellent communication, and a customer-centric attitude.

Iterating and Scaling Up

Iterating and scaling up is an ongoing and dynamic process that entails improving your product, streamlining processes, and growing your firm to accommodate growth. It comprises adjusting and upgrading your strategy in response to client feedback, market dynamics, and changing company requirements. Let's take a slow and easy approach to this concept:

Once your product or service has been launched, it is critical to iterate and enhance depending on customer feedback and market information. Gather input from your consumers on a regular basis through surveys, user testing, and support contacts. Analyze the input to discover areas for improvement, new features to consider, and problems to solve.

Iterate on your product or service based on the insights gathered from consumer feedback. This might include improving the user interface, adding new features, or enhancing speed. Changes that correspond with your product plan and have the greatest impact on customer happiness and value should be prioritized.

Maintain an agile mentality and strategy as you iterate. Adopt a test-and-learn mindset in which you try out new ideas, assess their impact, and iterate depending on the outcomes. Iterate in tiny, reasonable steps to reduce disturbance and allow for quick adaption.

Focus on expanding up your operations at the same time to handle rising demand and business development. This might include increasing your manufacturing capacity, streamlining your supply chain, or investing in new resources such as staff, equipment, or technology. Ascertain that your operations can handle increasing volume while preserving quality and customer satisfaction.

Monitor key performance indicators (KPIs) as you scale to track the efficacy of your efforts. Metrics such as revenue growth, client acquisition, retention rates, and operational efficiency should be measured. Assess these KPIs on a regular basis to evaluate the performance of your scaling activities and discover areas for additional development.

Scaling up frequently entails growing your market reach and client base, in addition to product and operational improvements. Consider branching out into new market sectors, geographic locations, or client demographics. Create focused marketing tactics and sales activities to attract and acquire new consumers while nurturing existing ones.

It is critical to retain a strong focus on client experience and happiness as you iterate and grow. Listen to your clients on a regular basis, understand their changing needs, and provide value that surpasses their expectations. Personalized communication, exceptional assistance, and a customer-centric attitude will help you build solid client connections.

Adopt a culture of constant development and learning inside your company. Encourage cross-functional cooperation, exchange of expertise, and experimentation. Encourage team members to feel empowered to share ideas, take chances, and learn from both triumphs and mistakes.

Keep in mind that iterating and scaling up is a continuous process. As your company grows and the market changes, you must continue to iterate, optimize, and expand in order to remain competitive and satisfy the changing demands of your consumers. You may achieve long-term success and promote sustainable development by constantly refining your product and strategically increasing your business.

Chapter 6: Marketing and Growth Strategies

Defining Your Target Market

Identifying your target market is a critical step in creating a successful marketing plan and reaching the correct audience for your product or service. It entails finding and comprehending the exact group of people or businesses who are most likely to be interested in what you have to offer. Let's take a slow and easy approach to this concept:

Begin by assessing your product or service and its unique value proposition in order to establish your target market. Take into account its characteristics, benefits, and the problem it answers. This knowledge will assist you in identifying the major traits and wants of clients who will find value in what you offer.

Following that, undertake market research to obtain insight into the larger market landscape. To determine the size and dynamics of your possible target market, investigate industry trends, consumer behavior, and rivals. This study assists you in identifying opportunities and refining your posture.

Segment your target market into distinct groups based on demographics, psychographics, behavior, or other relevant characteristics. Age, gender, geography, and income are all examples of demographics. Interests, values, lifestyle, and attitudes are all examples of psychographics. Customer activities, purchase habits, and use behavior are the subject of behavioral segmentation.

Create buyer personas, which are fictitious representations of your ideal clients in each target market group. These personas assist you understand your target audience's motives, pain areas, and preferences by humanizing them. This knowledge enables you to personalize your marketing messages and approaches to each persona.

Consider doing surveys, interviews, or focus groups to obtain direct feedback and insights from your target market. This primary research aids in the validation of assumptions, the discovery of unmet needs, and the refinement of your understanding of client preferences.

Monitor and evaluate your target market on a regular basis, since it may change over time. Market dynamics, trends, and client preferences can all shift, necessitating an adjustment to your target market definition. Keep an eye out for developing possibilities or trends in your target market by paying attention to feedback, client behavior, and market research.

Align your marketing efforts as you narrow your target market. Create captivating communications that appeal directly to your target audience's wants and objectives. Choose the most successful communication methods to reach and engage people, such as social media, internet advertising, events, or conventional media.

Keep in mind that your target market is not a static entity. It is a dynamic and ever-changing group of people or enterprises. Evaluate your marketing methods on a regular basis, examine client feedback, and adjust your approaches as needed to guarantee your efforts stay relevant and effective.

You can focus your marketing efforts, develop more compelling message, and make better relationships with the correct audience by identifying your target market. Understanding your target market's wants and traits helps you to adjust your products, services, and marketing activities to fit their individual needs, resulting in higher customer satisfaction and economic success.

Creating a Compelling Brand Identity

Developing a strong brand identity is akin to writing a one-of-a-kind and intriguing novel that captures the soul of your company. It entails identifying who you are, what you stand for, and how you want your target audience to view you. Let's explore this idea using a loose and continuous text:

Consider your brand to be a fictional character with its own personality, beliefs, and voice. Begin with identifying your brand's mission and why it exists other than to make a profit. What issue does your brand address? What value does it provide to people's lives? This mission statement serves as the cornerstone for your brand's identification.

Consider your target audience next. Who exactly are they? What are their wants, objectives, and goals? Customize your brand identity to connect with them on a deeper level. To establish an emotional connection, consider their demographics, psychographics, and habits. Your brand should have the sense of a trustworthy friend or mentor who understands and supports them.

Define the values and personality aspects of your brand. What do you hold dear? What distinguishes your brand and sets it apart from competitors? Incorporate these ideals throughout all aspects of your brand's experience. Allow your brand personality to come through in your goods, customer service, and marketing to develop an emotional relationship with your audience.

Create a captivating brand narrative that embodies your mission, beliefs, and differentiating selling proposition. Make it fascinating and real, catching your audience's attention and curiosity. Your tale should transport them on an emotional journey and leave a lasting impact. Make your brand memorable and relevant by using narrative tactics.

Brand identity is heavily reliant on visual components. Create a visually attractive logo, use colors that convey the right feelings, and use typefaces that match the nature of your company. Consistency in graphic components across all touchpoints strengthens and makes your brand easily recognized.

Create a brand voice and message that matches the personality of your company. Determine if you want to interact with your audience in a pleasant, professional, or fun manner. Create messaging that clearly and truly communicates your brand's value proposition. Your brand voice should connect with your target audience and resonate with them.

To develop a strong brand identity, you must honestly embody it. Maintain consistency in your brand experience by ensuring that your claims correspond to the actual consumer experience. Build trust and loyalty by engaging your audience in a true and open manner.

Be willing to adapt your brand identification as your company grows and the market changes. Maintain your responsiveness to client input, industry changes, and new possibilities. Evaluate the success of your brand identity on a regular basis and make changes to maintain it relevant and attractive.

Developing an engaging brand identity is a continual process. It is about constantly improving and growing your story in order for it to resonate with your target audience. You can develop a strong presence, generate client loyalty, and differentiate yourself in the market by creating a distinctive and true brand identity.

Developing a Comprehensive Marketing Plan

Creating a thorough marketing plan is like to navigating a route across a wide sea of chances in order to efficiently reach your target audience. It entails researching your market, creating goals, developing strategies, and putting them into action in order to promote your brand and fulfill your company objectives. Let's take a slow and easy approach to this concept:

Market Analysis:

Begin by doing an in-depth examination of your target market. Understand your target audience's demographics, psychographics, and habits. Determine market trends, competitors, and business possibilities. This study provides you with information about your clients' wants, preferences, and trouble spots.

Set Specific, Measurable, attainable, Relevant, and Time-Bound Goals:

Define specific, measurable, attainable, relevant, and time-bound (SMART) goals for your marketing activities. Clarity on your objectives helps you to coordinate your initiatives and quantify performance, whether it's raising brand recognition, generating sales, or gaining market share.

Create tailored plans:

Create tailored marketing plans based on your market analysis and goals. Determine the most effective routes for reaching your target audience, whether through digital marketing, social media, content marketing, advertising, public relations, or a mix of strategies. Adapt your techniques to your target audience's tastes and actions.

Define Your USP (Unique Selling Proposition):

Clearly describe your USP, which distinguishes you from rivals and emphasizes the distinct value you provide. Determine the primary features and benefits of your products or services that will appeal to your target audience. This helps to distinguish your brand in a congested market.

Implement Actionable Tactics:

Implement tactical efforts to successfully execute your marketing objectives. This might include content development, social media campaigns, SEO, email marketing, influencer collaborations, event attendance, or other applicable approaches. Select methods that are appropriate for your audience, goals, and available resources.

Create a Budget:

Create a budget for your marketing operations. Consider your objectives, expected outcomes, and the competitive environment. Determine the efficacy and return on investment (ROI) of various marketing channels and approaches. Review and alter your budget as needed on a regular basis.

Make a Content strategy:

Create a content strategy that is in line with your marketing strategies. Determine the form of material that is most appealing to your target audience, whether it be blog posts, videos, infographics, or podcasts. To guarantee constant and interesting content delivery, create a content schedule that includes themes, formats, and distribution methods.

Monitor, Measure, and Adjust:

Track the effectiveness of your marketing initiatives on a regular basis. Key metrics and key performance indicators (KPIs) include website traffic, conversion rates, social media engagement, lead generation, and customer acquisition expenses. Analyze the data to determine the efficacy of your strategy and approaches. To optimize results, adjust your plan depending on the insights gathered.

Develop Relationships and Engagement:

Concentrate on developing relationships with your target audience. Engage them in meaningful conversations, react to queries quickly, and solicit feedback. To nurture leads and establish client loyalty, use customer relationship management (CRM) technologies and strategies.

Maintain agility and adaptability:

Marketing is an ever-changing industry. Maintain agility and adapt to market, consumer, and technological developments. Monitor market developments, customer behavior, and emerging prospects on a regular basis. Be willing to experiment, learn from your mistakes, and fine-tune your marketing strategy accordingly.

Create a comprehensive and appealing brand messaging structure that consistently delivers your business's value proposition across all marketing platforms. Create key statements that are appealing to your target audience and clearly communicate the advantages of your products or services. Make sure your brand message corresponds to your unique selling proposition and brand identity.

Data and Analytics:

Use data and analytics to acquire insights into your marketing performance. Key indicators should be measured and analyzed to determine what is working and what needs to be improved. Track website traffic, marketing performance, consumer behavior, and ROI using tools and platforms. Make data-driven decisions using these insights to enhance your marketing campaigns.

Targeted Advertising:

Consider running targeted advertising campaigns to reach out to certain audience segments. To offer targeted messages to the appropriate individuals at the right time, use platforms such as Google Ads, social network advertising, or programmatic advertising. Adjust your targeting parameters depending on performance data to optimize your ad campaigns.

Invest in Content Marketing:

Use content marketing to attract, engage, and educate your target audience. Create meaningful and relevant material that targets your audience's problem areas and delivers solutions, such as blog articles, videos, e-books, or podcasts. Distribute this information over several media to generate thought leadership and trust with your audience.

Improve Customer Relationships:

Focus on developing strong client connections via individualized interactions and great customer service. To encourage customer loyalty and advocacy, implement techniques like as loyalty programs, referral programs, and customer feedback loops. Encourage favorable word-of-mouth recommendations and use client testimonials to boost the reputation of your brand.

Cooperate with Influencers:

Identify and cooperate with relevant influencers in your industry or specialty to broaden your reach and reputation. Engage influencers who share your brand's values and target demographic. To get into their engaged audience and build brand exposure, collaborate with them on product reviews, sponsored content, or co-created initiatives.

Actively monitor and respond to consumer feedback via social media, online reviews, and customer surveys. Respond to both good and negative feedback immediately and professionally to demonstrate that you respect consumer input. Utilize feedback to enhance your goods, services, and overall client experience.

Stay Ahead of the Competition:

Conduct frequent competitive analysis to stay current on industry trends, rival strategies, and new prospects. Identify places where you can differentiate yourself and possible market gaps. Use this knowledge to improve your marketing strategy and keep your competitive edge.

Stay Agile and Experiment:

Adopt an agile mentality and be open to new ideas. To find out what works best for your brand, try out fresh marketing channels, message techniques, or campaign methods. Learn from both triumphs and mistakes, iterate rapidly, and fine-tune your marketing strategy based on real-time data.

Review and update your marketing plan on a regular basis to stay current and respond to changing market conditions. Assess the success of your marketing initiatives on a regular basis, alter strategy as appropriate, and look for new ways to maximize your marketing efforts.

You may successfully promote your brand, interact with your target audience, and drive company growth by creating a thorough marketing plan and implementing smart activities. To remain ahead of the competition and reach your marketing goals, keep adaptable, assess results, and constantly adjust your methods.

Implementing Digital Marketing Strategies

Implementing digital marketing techniques entails harnessing the power of internet platforms to successfully reach and engage your target audience. It includes a wide variety of actions, from building a strong online presence to leveraging data-driven insights for improvement.

To begin, create an online presence by developing a professional website that matches your brand's identity and provides a streamlined user experience. Improve your website's exposure and organic traffic by optimizing it for search engines. This includes using relevant keywords, producing high-quality content, and optimizing website load times.

Content marketing is essential in digital marketing. Create a content plan that is in line with the interests and demands of your target audience. Create meaningful and entertaining material for your target audience, such as blog articles, videos, infographics, or podcasts, that educates, entertains, or solves problems. Distribute your material across several channels, such as your website, social media platforms, email newsletters, or industry journals.

Make use of social media networks to engage with your target audience and raise brand recognition. Determine which channels your target audience prefers and develop compelling social media content that stimulates participation, sharing, and comments. Develop relationships with your followers by responding to their comments and queries in a timely and genuine manner.

Use search engine optimization (SEO) tactics to increase the visibility of your website in search engine results pages. Conduct keyword research to uncover relevant search phrases and optimize the content, meta tags, and URLs of your website accordingly. Concentrate on producing relevant and user-friendly material that corresponds to the purpose of search searches.

Paid advertising, such as pay-per-click (PPC) campaigns, can also be incorporated into your digital marketing plan. Target particular audiences and show ads based on their interests and habits using platforms such as Google Ads or social media advertising. Set specific goals for your ad campaigns, analyze their effectiveness on a regular basis, and improve them to maximize your return on investment (ROI).

Another effective digital marketing strategy is email marketing. Build an email list by providing your audience with relevant material or unique offers. Create tailored email campaigns to nurture prospects, increase client loyalty, and increase conversions. Marketing automation technologies can help you simplify your email marketing operations and send relevant messages to the right people at the right time.

Data-driven insights should be included into your digital marketing plan. Monitor and evaluate key performance indicators (KPIs) like as website traffic, conversion rates, engagement metrics, and consumer behavior using analytics tools. This information allows you to assess the efficacy of your marketing efforts, find areas for development, and make data-driven decisions to improve your campaigns.

Keep up with industry developments, new technology, and changes in customer behavior. To stay current and ahead of the competition, you must constantly modify and develop your digital marketing techniques. Experiment with different methods and channels, do A/B tests, and learn from both triumphs and mistakes.

Keep in mind that digital marketing is a dynamic and ever-changing sector. Continue to be nimble, experiment, and use the potential of digital platforms to engage with your target audience, increase brand recognition, and achieve your marketing objectives.

Measuring and Optimizing Growth

Measuring and optimizing growth is a continuous process that entails tracking important indicators, evaluating data, and making strategic changes to support corporate success. It's like navigating a twisting route, continuously assessing your progress and making course changes along the way.

To begin, identify the essential KPIs that are most important to your company goals. Revenue, customer acquisition cost (CAC), conversion rates, client retention, and any other relevant performance data might be included. You receive significant insights into the health and success of your firm by explicitly defining and measuring key KPIs.

Data may be collected and analyzed from a variety of sources, including sales records, website analytics, customer feedback, and marketing initiatives. Make use of tools and platforms that assist you in successfully gathering and organizing data. The study will show patterns, trends, and areas for improvement that can help you plan your next steps in growing your business.

By delving deeper into the data, you can identify growth prospects. Examine trends and correlations to identify places where you may improve performance or grow your consumer base. Identify bottlenecks or hurdles to growth and devise solutions to overcome them. To discover possible opportunities, consider market trends, consumer input, and competitor analyses.

Experiment with different growth plans and approaches. Use A/B testing to examine alternative tactics and determine what works best for your company. Iterate and modify your strategy in response to data-driven insights. Maintain an open mind and a willingness to accept new ideas and adapt to changing market conditions.

Create a culture of continual development inside your company. Encourage team cooperation and information sharing to generate new ideas and creative solutions. Create a welcoming atmosphere in which workers feel empowered to suggest and carry out development projects.

Evaluate the impact of your optimizations and modifications on a regular basis. To determine the efficacy of your efforts, compare the results to your set KPIs. Identify areas where you have had success and places where you may need to improve.

Maintain flexibility and responsiveness to market developments. Monitor industry developments, consumer behavior, and the competitive environment on a regular basis to uncover new growth prospects. Keep an eye out for future technologies and digital breakthroughs that might provide new methods to reach and engage your target audience.

Keep in mind that assessing and optimizing growth is a continuous activity. Adopt a philosophy of constant learning and growth. Be prepared to take measured chances, learn from both triumphs and mistakes, and change your methods as needed.

You can promote sustainable development for your organization by continuously evaluating important indicators, analyzing data, and making educated adjustments. Maintaining focus, adaptability, and responsiveness to market conditions can position your company for long-term success.

Chapter 7: Managing Operations and Scaling Up

Establishing Efficient Processes and Systems

Creating effective procedures and systems is akin to creating a well-oiled machine that increases output, reduces waste, and promotes seamless operations inside your company. It entails simplifying procedures, integrating automation, and optimizing resource use to achieve maximum efficiency. Let's take a slow and easy approach to this concept:

Begin by assessing your current procedures and finding opportunities for improvement. Examine for bottlenecks, redundancies, and inefficiencies that might be impeding productivity. This assessment assists you in determining where to concentrate your efforts for process optimization.

Workflows may be streamlined by sketching out each stage of a process and identifying opportunities to reduce redundant jobs or streamline communication channels. Simplify complicated procedures, define roles and responsibilities, and make sure everyone knows their involvement in the entire process.

Consider using automation and technology to automate repetitive or time-consuming operations. Make use of software, tools, and systems that can automate data input, reporting, communication, and other manual tasks. This allows your staff to focus on more value-added operations.

Ensure uniformity and efficiency across departments or teams by standardizing processes. Make clear and easy-to-understand paperwork outlining step-by-step methods, guidelines, and best practices. This enables personnel to adhere to defined practices, reducing mistakes and confusion.

Improve cooperation, coordination, and task management by implementing efficient project management approaches. Use project management software or tools that allow for precise work assignment, progress monitoring, and effective communication. This guarantees that projects are completed on schedule and within budget.

Using key performance indicators (KPIs), continuously monitor and measure process performance. Measure variables like cycle time, throughput, mistake rates, and customer satisfaction to determine how effective your operations are. Based on these findings, identify areas that require more optimization or change.

Encourage an organizational culture of continual improvement. Encourage open communication and feedback loops so that staff may offer process improvements or share creative ideas. Allow workers to own their workflows and participate to process optimization.

Invest in staff training and development to ensure they have the skills and knowledge needed to do their jobs effectively. Give them the tools and resources they need to succeed in their duties. Provide continuing assistance and mentoring to assist them in efficiently navigating difficult processes.

Review and adjust your procedures on a regular basis to react to changing business demands or market conditions. In order to get insights into process pain points or developing requirements, solicit input from workers and stakeholders. Continuously look for ways to increase the efficiency of processes and systems.

You may boost production, save expenses, and create a more streamlined and successful business by using efficient procedures and systems. Adopt a continuous improvement approach, make use of technology and automation, and empower your staff to participate to the optimization process. You'll be well-positioned to promote development, provide excellent customer experiences, and achieve operational excellence if you have effective procedures in place.

Managing Cash Flow and Resources

Managing cash flow and resources is akin to navigating your company's financial waters in order to maintain a healthy and sustainable operation. It entails successfully monitoring and regulating the flow of funds into and out of your firm while improving resource use. Let's take a slow and easy approach to this concept:

Creating a detailed budget and financial projection is the first step in cash flow management. Determine your income streams and project your expenses, including operational costs, inventory, overhead, and debt commitments. This gives you a clear view of your anticipated cash inflows and outflows.

Regularly monitor your cash flow to guarantee enough liquidity. Keep track of your cash inflows and outflows from sales, investments, and financing operations, as well as your costs and investments. You may meet your financial responsibilities and capture development possibilities by maintaining a healthy cash flow and properly managing your working capital.

Improve your cash flow management methods, such as streamlining your billing and collection operations. To avoid payment delays, invoice immediately and follow up on pending payments. To speed up the collection process, consider giving incentives for early payment or utilizing automated payment solutions.

Controlling expenditures and optimizing resource allocation can help you manage your spending intelligently. Review your running expenditures on a regular basis to find areas where you may cut excessive spending or negotiate better terms with suppliers. Implement cost-cutting methods without sacrificing product or service quality.

Maintain a reserve money to cover unexpected costs or financial issues. Having a cash reserve may act as a safety net during difficult times or unanticipated events, providing business continuity and financial stability.

Optimize your resource consumption by detecting inefficiencies and figuring out how to get the most out of your assets. This involves managing inventory levels effectively to reduce carrying costs and decreasing surplus or outdated inventory. Examine your workforce requirements to ensure that you have the proper people to support your business operations without incurring needless costs.

Consider strategic alliances or outsourcing options to tap into other resources and skills. This enables you to gain access to particular talents or capabilities without making large upfront costs. To improve resource allocation, do a cost-benefit analysis of outsourcing certain tasks vs maintaining them in-house.

Review and evaluate financial statements on a regular basis to acquire insight into your company's financial health. Understand important financial measures and indicators including liquidity, profitability, and solvency. These measures assist you in assessing overall financial performance and making sound judgments about resource allocation and growth plans.

Maintain constant contact with lenders, suppliers, and other critical stakeholders. Build excellent relationships and negotiate advantageous terms to help you with your cash flow management activities. Address any possible concerns or challenges ahead of time to guarantee a seamless flow of resources.

Revisit and revise your cash flow estimate and budget on a regular basis to reflect changes in your company environment. Monitor and adapt your tactics on a regular basis to maximize cash flow and resource management.

You can secure your company's financial stability and sustainability by successfully managing cash flow and resources. Maintain a healthy cash flow, keep expenses under control, maximize resource usage, and make sound financial judgments. You can negotiate problems, capture opportunities, and position your organization for long-term success with smart financial management.

Scaling Up Production and Operations

Scaling up production and operations is similar to extending your company's capacity to satisfy rising demand and capture new possibilities. To promote business expansion, it entails boosting production capacity, streamlining processes, and improving operational efficiency. Let's take a slow and easy approach to this concept:

Scaling up manufacturing becomes necessary when your company grows to satisfy rising client demand. Examine your present production capacity and discover areas that need to be expanded or improved. This might entail purchasing new equipment, recruiting more trained workers, or improving existing procedures.

Optimize your workflows to guarantee that your operations run smoothly and efficiently. Analyze each phase of your manufacturing process to uncover bottlenecks or inefficiencies and strategies to simplify operations. Look for ways to automate repetitive operations, use lean manufacturing concepts, and enhance overall material and information flow.

Examine your supply network and make changes to accommodate additional output. Improve supplier relationships, negotiate advantageous terms, and maintain a consistent and timely supply of raw materials or components. To reduce risks and increase flexibility, consider diversifying your supply base.

Increase operational efficiency by investing in technology and digital solutions. Optimize production planning, inventory management, and quality control by implementing enterprise resource planning (ERP) systems, manufacturing execution systems (MES), or other software solutions. Analyze data to acquire insights into production performance and discover opportunities for improvement.

Create a trained staff that can handle growing production needs. Determine any skill shortages in your present personnel. Provide staff with chances for training and growth, or consider acquiring new personnel with the relevant experience. To strengthen operational capabilities, foster a culture of continual learning and growth.

Check that your infrastructure and facilities can handle the increasing production demands. To handle expanding activities, evaluate your physical space, equipment, and utilities. Consider whether you need to update or invest in new buildings, machinery, or technology to fulfill your company's rising demands.

Establish stringent quality control techniques to ensure that product standards are maintained as manufacturing ramps up. To maintain consistency and customer satisfaction, implement quality assurance methods, conduct frequent inspections, and monitor product performance. Improve your quality management systems on a regular basis to reduce faults and improve the client experience.

To guarantee smooth logistics and distribution, review and update your supply chain management plans. Improve inventory management to reduce carrying costs while satisfying client requests. Investigate relationships with third-party logistics companies or explore building your own distribution network to effectively reach new markets.

Track key performance indicators (KPIs) to determine the effectiveness of your scaling initiatives. Monitor parameters like as output, cycle time, inventory turnover, customer satisfaction, and operational expenses. Analyze these indicators on a regular basis to find areas for further improvement and make data-driven decisions.

To foresee future growth potential, keep an eye on market trends, client requests, and industry advances. To react to shifting market circumstances, you must constantly innovate and remain adaptable. Encourage a culture of continuous improvement to promote innovation, increase productivity, and fuel long-term success.

You can satisfy rising client demand, capitalize on new possibilities, and expand your business by properly scaling up production and operations. To ensure effective and sustainable operations on a larger scale, continuously improve workflows, invest in technology, grow your employees, and analyze performance.

Streamlining Supply Chain and Logistics

Streamlining the supply chain and logistics entails maximizing the seamless and efficient flow of goods, information, and services from suppliers to customers. It's similar to choreographing a well-choreographed dance in which every step is synced and harmonized.

Begin by assessing your supply chain procedures and identifying opportunities for improvement. Look identify bottlenecks, redundant processes, and inefficiencies that may be eliminated. Map out the full supply chain to get a complete picture of how supplies, information, and financial transactions move.

Utilize data-driven strategies to improve inventory management. Analyze demand trends, using forecasting methodologies, and establish ideal inventory levels to reduce stockouts or surplus inventory. To track and manage inventory more efficiently, use technology like as inventory management systems or RFID tagging.

Improve supplier relationships by encouraging open communication and collaboration. Set clear expectations, negotiate advantageous conditions, and form long-term alliances. Evaluate supplier performance on a regular basis and look for chances for continual improvement.

Use technology to improve visibility and transparency across the supply chain. Implement supply chain management solutions that integrate data from multiple stakeholders, allowing for real-time visibility into inventory levels, manufacturing schedules, and transportation status. This allows for proactive decision-making and effective coordination.

To minimize waste and increase operational efficiency, embrace lean concepts and continuous improvement approaches.

Processes should be streamlined, needless procedures eliminated, and people should be empowered to find and address inefficiencies. Track progress by regularly monitoring performance measures such as lead time, cycle time, and order correctness.

To optimize transportation and distribution procedures, work with logistics partners. To cut costs and shorten delivery times, evaluate shipping routes, combine goods, and use freight optimization technologies. Adopt sustainable logistics techniques to lower your carbon impact and achieve environmental goals.

To maintain product integrity and customer happiness, implement stringent quality control methods across the supply chain. Conduct frequent inspections, follow stringent testing processes, and set quality targets. Monitor and enhance product and process quality on an ongoing basis to reduce faults and customer complaints.

Utilize data analytics and predictive modeling to forecast demand, improve production schedules, and effectively manage inventories. Use data from several sources to spot patterns, trends, and opportunities for improvement. To acquire actionable insights and make educated decisions, use sophisticated analytics technologies.

Encourage cross-functional supply chain collaboration and communication. Dismantle silos and cultivate a collaborative mentality across various departments or stakeholders. This allows for greater synchronization, faster problem solving, and overall performance improvement.

Review and adjust your supply chain strategy on a regular basis to respond to changing market conditions and client expectations. Keep up to date on industry trends, emerging technology, and regulatory developments that may have an influence on your supply chain. Continuously look for methods to improve and optimize your supply chain procedures.

You may save money, boost customer happiness, and gain a competitive advantage by optimizing your supply chain and logistics. Improve coordination, take use of technology, fortify connections, and promote a culture of continual development. You can deliver items to clients faster, cut operating costs, and improve overall business performance with a well-optimized supply chain.

Monitoring and Adjusting Business Performance

Monitoring and modifying company performance is analogous to sailing a ship on a continuously shifting sea, where you maintain a keen eye on the horizon, analyze current conditions, and make timely modifications to stay on course towards your objectives. It entails regularly monitoring important indicators, evaluating data, and adjusting methods to improve performance and accomplish desired results. Let's take a slow and easy approach to this concept:

Begin by identifying the key performance indicators (KPIs) that correspond to your company goals. Financial measurements, customer satisfaction scores, sales objectives, and operational efficiency indicators are examples of these. Choose metrics that give useful insights into various elements of your company's success.

Monitor and measure these KPIs on a regular basis to acquire a comprehensive knowledge of your company's success. Collect, organize, and display important data using technology and data analytics techniques. This allows you to take snapshots of your performance in real time or on a regular basis and spot trends, patterns, or abnormalities.

Analyze the data to learn about your company's strengths, weaknesses, opportunities, and dangers. Identify areas where you thrive and places where you need to develop. Look for patterns, correlations, or causal linkages that may indicate underlying issues affecting your performance.

Determine opportunities for improvement or optimization based on your study. Create action plans to fix shortcomings and capitalize on possibilities. Marketing tactics may be refined, pricing models adjusted, product offers enhanced, or operational procedures optimized.

Review and update your business strategy and plans on a regular basis to respond to changing market conditions or evolving client wants. Adopt an agile and flexible culture that allows you to adapt quickly to new possibilities or obstacles.

Communicate your findings and potential changes to your team to ensure alignment and a collaborative approach. Encourage workers to share their perspectives, thoughts, and proposals for improvements. Adopt an attitude of continual learning that encourages creativity and develops an improvement culture.

Changes should be implemented and the influence on business performance should be monitored. Keep track of the outcomes of your modifications and compare them to your planned outcomes. Assess the success of your strategy and activities, and make changes as needed to improve performance.

Update stakeholders on business performance on a regular basis, such as workers, investors, or consumers. Transparently communicating progress, difficulties, and accomplishments fosters trust and keeps everyone up to date.

Keep up to date on industry trends, upcoming technology, and the competitive environment. Benchmark your performance against industry standards or best practices on a regular basis. Look for ways to learn from successful peers and apply their tactics to your own situation.

Adopt an attitude of constant development and innovation. Encourage risk-taking and experimentation, and learn from both triumphs and mistakes. Create an atmosphere in which learning from mistakes is valued and used as a springboard for advancement.

You may guide your company toward success by regularly assessing and changing its performance. Maintain vigilance, assess data, change techniques, and build an improvement culture. This allows you to overcome obstacles, capitalize on opportunities, and achieve your company goals.

Chapter 8: Navigating Challenges and Overcoming Obstacles

Managing Uncertainty and Risk

Managing uncertainty and risk is similar to starting on an unknown voyage, where you foresee probable problems, establish contingency plans, and make educated decisions to limit negative consequences. It entails detecting, analyzing, and managing risks in order to preserve company continuity, safeguard assets, and capitalize on opportunities in a volatile and unpredictable environment. Let's take a slow and easy approach to this concept:

Identify possible threats:

Begin by identifying possible threats to your firm. Financial risks, operational risks, legal and compliance risks, and market risks are examples of internal or external risks. Encourage open communication and collaboration among your team members in order to discover possible dangers from many angles.

Assess Risk Impact and Likelihood:

Assess each detected risk's possible impact and likelihood. Consider the gravity of the repercussions, their likelihood of occurrence, and the period within which they may occur. This aids in risk prioritization and resource allocation.

Create Risk Mitigation measures:

Once hazards have been identified and analyzed, create suitable risk mitigation measures. Implementing preventive steps, developing contingency plans, diversifying suppliers or markets, or obtaining insurance coverage are all examples. Depending on the circumstances, try to establish a balance between risk avoidance, risk transfer, and risk acceptance.

Monitor and Evaluate:

Continuously monitor the identified risks and evaluate their efficacy on a regular basis. Keep up to date on changes in the business landscape, industry trends, and regulatory requirements that may affect your risk profile. Change your strategy as needed to accommodate new threats or shifting priorities.

Foster a Risk-Aware Culture:

Spread a risk-awareness and responsibility culture across your firm. Encourage staff to report any hazards or difficulties as soon as possible, and make open communication channels available. Educate and teach your staff on risk management methods, providing them with the information and skills they need to successfully detect and respond to hazards.

Scenario Planning and Stress Testing:

Conduct scenario planning exercises and stress testing to examine your company's resilience under various risk scenarios. Evaluate your readiness and reaction capacities by simulating probable interruptions or crises. This assists in identifying vulnerabilities and fine-tuning risk mitigation techniques.

Engage External Expertise:

Consider bringing in outside help to help with your risk management initiatives. Consultants, industry experts, and legal specialists may all give significant insights and advice on unique dangers to your organization. To keep updated about best practices and new hazards, join professional networks or industry groups.

Review and Update:

Review and update your risk management plans on a regular basis to adapt to changing conditions. Conduct periodic risk assessments, appraise risk impact and likelihood, and analyze the efficacy of risk mitigation strategies. Maintain a proactive and responsive approach to new hazards that may arise over time.

Stakeholder Engagement and contact:

Maintain open and proactive contact with stakeholders like as workers, customers, investors, and suppliers. Maintain regular communication with them on your risk management initiatives, crisis response strategies, and any possible impacts on their interests. Develop ties with important stakeholders in order to develop teamwork and obtain support during difficult times.

Embrace possibilities:

While managing risks, keep an eye out for prospective possibilities. Examine the risk-reward trade-offs and decide whether taking reasonable risks matches with your strategic goals. A risk-management strategy that is well-executed may lead to innovation, growth, and a competitive edge.

Reflect on Previous Experiences:

Reflect on previous experiences and learn from both achievements and disappointments. Analyze how risks were managed, what worked effectively, and where improvements may be made. Utilize these insights to improve your risk management and decision-making processes. Encourage an organizational culture of constant learning and progress.

Accept Agile Decision-Making:

Adopt agile decision-making methods in an uncertain and fast changing environment. Be adaptable and responsive, allowing for fast changes and revisions as new data becomes available. Encourage a decentralized decision-making culture by allowing workers at all levels to make informed decisions within their areas of competence.

Anticipate and Plan for Different Scenarios:

Anticipate several probable scenarios and create contingency plans for each. Think about the best-case, worst-case, and most likely scenarios. This allows you to plan for a variety of scenarios and make educated decisions in real time when unexpected occurrences occur.

Develop Strong Stakeholder ties:

Develop strong ties with important stakeholders like as customers, suppliers, partners, and regulators. Open channels of communication and cooperation build confidence and allow for a group response to risk management concerns. To obtain varied viewpoints and ideas, engage in continuing debate, solicit feedback, and include stakeholders in decision-making processes.

Utilize Technology and Data Analytics:

Take advantage of technology and data analytics to improve your risk management skills. To detect possible hazards and trends, use sophisticated risk assessment tools, automate data collection and analysis, and apply predictive analytics. Utilize developing technologies such as artificial intelligence and machine learning to acquire a better understanding of risk trends and improve risk mitigation techniques.

Stay Informed and Agile:

Keep up to current on market developments, regulatory changes, and new hazards that may affect your organization. Monitor external circumstances that may have an impact on your risk landscape. Adopt an agile mentality to help you to swiftly adjust to new problems and capitalize on emerging possibilities.

Establish clear and effective communication channels within your business to convey risk-related information. Make sure staff have access to risk management information, rules, and practices. Encourage staff to report hazards or concerns in a timely manner by fostering open and honest communication.

Regular risk assessments should be carried out in order to proactively identify and analyze possible dangers. Consider both internal and external elements that may have an influence on your company, such as economic conditions, technology breakthroughs, or geopolitical events. Regular evaluations allow you to anticipate developing hazards and establish proactive risk mitigation methods.

Continuously Improve:

Adopt an attitude of continuous improvement and look for chances to improve your risk management methods. Encourage comments and recommendations from workers and stakeholders in order to foster an environment of creativity and learning. Review and assess the efficiency of your risk management systems on a regular basis, adjusting them to adapt to changing conditions.

Embrace Resilience and Adaptability:

Build adaptive capability and the ability to recover from setbacks within your business to foster resilience. Create a culture that welcomes change, fosters learning from mistakes, and adjusts rapidly to new situations. Create contingency plans and redundancies as needed to improve your capacity to withstand and recover from disruptive occurrences.

You can navigate uncertainty with confidence, protect your organization, and embrace opportunities by using effective risk management procedures. Adopt a proactive, agile strategy, make use of technology and data analytics, and cultivate a culture of continuous improvement. You can better handle risks and position your firm for long-term success if you have strong risk management measures in place.

Adapting to Changing Market Conditions

Adapting to shifting market conditions is like riding a wave that moves and alters all the time. To traverse the ever-changing currents of consumer needs, technology breakthroughs, and competitive landscapes, a flexible and fluid strategy is required. Let's take a slow and easy approach to this concept:

Staying adaptive is critical in today's volatile business world. It all starts with staying on top of market developments, client preferences, and new possibilities. Analyze market research, customer insights, and competitor activity on a regular basis to acquire a complete picture of the shifting scene.

Be prepared to alter your strategy, business models, and product offers when market conditions change. Adopt an agile attitude in which you can adjust rapidly to evolving trends and capitalize on new possibilities. This might include narrowing your target market, expanding into new markets, or launching novel products and services.

Pay close attention to your consumers and collect feedback through numerous sources. Engage in meaningful discussions, conduct polls, and use social media channels to learn about their wants and needs. Adapt your solutions to match their changing needs and deliver unique customer experiences that distinguish your business.

Keep an eye on your rivals and learn from their achievements and mistakes. Keep up to date on their initiatives, product launches, and consumer interaction techniques. Determine market gaps or places where you can surpass your competition. Accept innovation, try new techniques, and seek to remain ahead of the competition.

Accept technology as a tool for adaptability. To gain insights, expedite operations, and improve decision-making, use digital technologies, data analytics, and automation. To satisfy the rising demands of digitally informed consumers, invest in digital marketing techniques, e-commerce capabilities, and customer relationship management systems.

Develop an organizational culture of innovation and continual learning. Encourage people to think creatively, try out new ideas, and question the existing quo. To encourage a dynamic and adaptable workforce, provide venues for cross-functional cooperation and information exchange.

Review and evaluate your performance on a regular basis using appropriate key performance indicators (KPIs). Keep an eye on measures like sales growth, client retention, market share, and profitability. This data-driven strategy gives insights into the efficacy of your tactics and enables you to make educated changes.

Create a feedback loop with your consumers and stakeholders to stay on top of changing requirements and preferences. Engage in communication, solicit feedback, and demonstrate a real desire to modify depending on their criticism. This customer-focused strategy fosters loyalty, improves connections, and positions your company for long-term success.

Adopt a philosophy of constant development and adaptability. Be proactive in looking for ways to improve your operations, streamline procedures, and increase efficiency. Encourage workers at all levels to share suggestions for improvement and to take ownership of driving change.

Finally, retain your resilience and endurance. Adapting to changing market conditions can be difficult, but it also opens up new chances for development and innovation. Accept change, accept uncertainty, and view it as a voyage of constant progress and learning.

You may prepare your firm for success by remaining versatile and sensitive to changing market conditions. Embrace flexibility, listen to your consumers, keep an eye on the competition, harness technology, and cultivate an innovative culture. You can surf the tides of change and direct your firm toward long-term success if you are constantly willing to adapt.

Dealing with Competition and Disruption

In today's fast-paced corporate scene, dealing with competition and disruption necessitates a flexible and adaptable attitude. It's similar to managing a crowded marketplace where new rivals arise, technologies advance, and customer tastes vary quickly.

To prosper in the face of competition and disruption, it is critical to have a mentality that views obstacles as opportunities for development and progress. Conduct rigorous market research, obtain consumer feedback, and analyze data to stay tuned in to the requirements and tastes of your target market. This knowledge enables you to better personalize your services and customer experience in order to surpass your competition.

Differentiation is essential. Create a distinct value proposition and brand identity that distinguishes you from the competition. Determine your brand's unique strengths, core capabilities, and significant differentiators. Effectively communicate your brand narrative, emphasizing the unique selling aspects that provide buyers a compelling reason to pick your products or services.

To stay ahead, you must constantly innovate. Develop a culture of innovation and creativity inside your firm. Encourage people to think outside the box, recognize and reward risk-taking, and invest in R&D. Keep an eye out for developing technology and market trends that might disrupt your sector. Maintain a competitive advantage through adapting new technology, procedures, and business models.

It is critical to be agile and adaptable. Improve your capacity to adapt quickly to market developments and disruptions. Develop a flexible organizational structure that enables speedy decision-making and effective resource allocation. Encourage cross-functional cooperation and provide staff the freedom to bring new ideas and solutions.

It is critical to cultivate good relationships. Develop good relationships with your customers, suppliers, and partners. Create client loyalty by providing outstanding service, unique experiences, and real connections. Collaborate with strategic partners to maximize mutual value by using each other's capabilities. Establish relationships and networks to broaden your reach and talents.

Maintain vigilance and keep an eye on the market for any disruptions. Be aware of developing trends, technology, and changing client wants. Create proactive contingency plans to reduce risks and capitalize on possibilities. Review and assess your company model and strategy on a regular basis to find vulnerabilities and possibilities for improvement.

Create a culture of ongoing learning and progress. Encourage staff to keep current on industry trends, to take part in professional development programs, and to share their expertise within the business. Seek input from consumers and stakeholders actively to identify areas for improvement and change your tactics accordingly.

Accept digital transformation as a tool for gaining a competitive advantage. To improve consumer interaction, streamline processes, and get insights into market trends, use digital technologies such as digital marketing, e-commerce platforms, data analytics, and automation tools. Accept digital transformation as a driver of development and resilience.

Ultimately, remaining customer-centric is critical. Put your clients at the forefront of your decision-making processes. Continue to listen to their input, solve their concerns, and go above and above their expectations. Anticipate their changing requirements and provide customized solutions that beat your competition. Building long-term connections built on trust and providing exceptional client experiences can distinguish your company and secure its success in a competitive and dynamic industry.

Building Resilience and Learning from Failure

Building resilience and learning from failure is akin to putting a spring in your step, allowing you to bounce back stronger and wiser when confronted with obstacles and setbacks. It entails adopting a mentality that views failure as an opportunity for progress, developing the ability to deal with adversity, and always improving based on lessons learned. Let's take a slow and easy approach to this concept:

The ability to adapt, recover, and prosper in the face of adversity is referred to as resilience. It begins with accepting failure as a natural part of the path to achievement. Instead of seeing failure as a hurdle, consider it a stepping stone toward improvement and creativity.

Take time after failures to reflect on what went wrong and identify the lessons learnt. Recognize that failure is not a reflection of your value or ability, but rather a chance to rethink your strategy, procedures, and judgments. Analyze the core reasons of failure and consider other methods to success.

Encourage workers to consider failure as a useful learning experience by cultivating a growth attitude inside your firm. Create a secure and supportive workplace in which people feel comfortable taking chances and expressing their shortcomings openly. To build a culture of continual learning and progress, encourage open communication, cooperation, and information sharing.

Develop a solid support network to help you build resilience. Surround yourself with mentors, advisers, and coworkers who can offer advice, support, and other viewpoints. Seek their advice and use their experiences to acquire insights and conquer challenges. Collaboration and support can help you overcome obstacles more effectively and create team resilience.

Prepare for foreseeable hazards and create contingency measures to limit their impact. Proactively identify possible risks and plan for unanticipated situations. This involves establishing backup plans, diversifying revenue streams, and preserving financial stability in the face of adversity.

Invest in personal and professional development to expand your knowledge and abilities. Learn about industry trends, upcoming technology, and best practices on a regular basis. Seek out training opportunities, attend conferences, and participate in networking events to extend your horizons and create resilience via knowledge and expertise.

Adopt an exploratory mentality that promotes invention and creativity. Accept a culture that encourages calculated risk-taking and recognizes both achievements and mistakes. Encourage staff to experiment with new ideas, prototype initiatives, and learn from the results. This iterative strategy enables ongoing development and the identification of new opportunities.

Recognize the significance of self-care and well-being in the development of resilience. Prioritize physical and mental health since they serve as the foundation for good decision-making and problem-solving. Encourage work-life balance, stress management practices, and support networks to guarantee your and your team's well-being.

Celebrate tiny victories and landmarks along the path. Recognize progress and accomplishments, no matter how minor, to increase morale and motivation. Recognize individual and team efforts and contributions to reinforce a healthy and resilient culture.

Remember that building resilience is a process that takes time. Accept failure as a learning opportunity, tap into support networks, engage in personal and professional development, and cultivate an environment of creativity and experimentation. You may bounce back stronger, adapt to change, and enjoy the route to long-term success by developing resilience and learning from mistakes.

Sustaining Long-Term Growth and Success

Maintaining long-term development and success is akin to cultivating a thriving ecology in which your company may thrive. It necessitates a comprehensive and adaptable strategy that includes all parts of your company. It entails constantly improving consumer value, encouraging innovation, and responding to changing market circumstances.

Prioritizing client value is critical for long-term growth. Keep an eye out for their wants, preferences, and feedback. Make every effort to give great products, services, and experiences that meet and exceed their expectations. Stay relevant and differentiate yourself in the market by always improving and innovating.

Develop an innovative culture inside your firm. Encourage innovation, experimentation, and the desire to question the current quo. Accept evolving technology and market trends as possibilities for development and progress. Create an atmosphere that views failure as a learning opportunity and promotes successful initiatives.

Maintain flexibility and adaptability in response to changing market conditions. Maintain an eye on industry developments, customer behavior, and the competitive environment. To keep ahead of the curve, be willing to change your tactics, product offers, and business structures. Accept change as a source of opportunity rather than a danger.

Invest in your skills and help them grow. Attract and keep qualified employees that share your company's values and goals. Provide training and development opportunities to help them reach their full potential. A motivated and trained team adds to your company's long-term success.

Form strategic alliances and collaborations to broaden your reach and skills. Find ways to partner with similar businesses, suppliers, and distributors. Use their knowledge, resources, and networks to boost your growth potential. Strategic collaborations can pave the way for new forms of innovation and market development.

Create efficient performance measuring techniques to monitor your development and success. Set specific goals and key performance indicators (KPIs) that are in line with your long-term aims. Monitor and assess your performance in relation to these measures on a regular basis. Make data-driven decisions and drive changes using the insights gathered.

Maintain contact with your stakeholders. Build trust and credibility by keeping your promises and keeping lines of communication open. Engage your customers, workers, suppliers, investors, and community members. To develop a favorable reputation, act properly while considering environmental and social factors.

Manage risks proactively and preserve company continuity. Develop comprehensive risk management techniques after identifying possible risks. Prepare contingency plans to address possible hazards and reduce interruptions. Keep up to date on regulatory changes and compliance requirements to minimize any negative impact on your business.

Accept sustainability as a fundamental value. Incorporate environmentally friendly methods into your company's operations, supply networks, and decision-making processes. In your strategy, consider environmental, social, and governance aspects. Meet the expectations of socially conscious consumers by demonstrating your commitment to ethical business operations.

Strive to be relevant and competitive at all times. Future trends, technology improvements, and client wants should all be anticipated. Invest in R&D in order to innovate and provide new solutions. To keep your competitive advantage, embrace a proactive strategy to modifying your goods, services, and business strategies.

Develop long-term connections with consumers, vendors, and stakeholders. By creating unique experiences, you can increase client retention and loyalty. Create long-lasting alliances based on mutual trust and similar goals. These long-term ties contribute to your company's long-term growth and success.

You may achieve long-term growth and success by using a comprehensive and flexible strategy. Prioritize customer value, encourage innovation, adjust to market changes, and cultivate strong partnerships. Monitor your performance on a regular basis, minimize risks, and embrace sustainability. This constant focus on development and adaptability will position your company for long-term success.

Chapter 9: Customer Acquisition and Retention Strategies

Attracting New Customers

Attracting new consumers is similar to throwing a wide net in order to capture the attention and interest of prospective purchasers. It entails putting in place plans and methods to highlight the value of your products or services and persuade prospects to select your brand over rivals. Let's take a slow and easy approach to this concept:

Understanding your consumers' wants, interests, and pain spots is critical for attracting new customers. Conduct market research and collect consumer feedback to acquire a comprehensive grasp of your target demographic. Determine their motivations, difficulties, and objectives so that your marketing messages and solutions may be tailored properly.

Create a compelling value proposition that highlights the distinct benefits and value that your products or services bring. Highlight the challenges you address, the benefits you provide, and the ways you distinguish from rivals. Create convincing marketing messaging that speak to your target clients' unique pain concerns.

To reach a larger audience, use a variety of marketing platforms and strategies. To increase your online visibility, use digital marketing tactics such as search engine optimization (SEO), pay-per-click (PPC) advertising, social media marketing, and content marketing. Traditional advertising strategies, such as print ads or radio commercials, should be considered if they are relevant to your target market.

Create engaging and useful content that will educate and engage your target audience. Publish blog posts, films, infographics, or podcasts that offer useful insights, answer frequently asked questions, or address industry concerns. To attract consumers looking for answers, establish yourself as a trusted authority in your sector.

Improve your exposure and attract organic visitors by optimizing your website and online presence. Make sure your website is user-friendly, visually appealing, and search engine optimized. Use search engine optimization tactics to enhance the ranking of your website in search results, making it simpler for potential consumers to find you.

Create referral programs or incentives for current customers to promote friends, family, or coworkers to your company. Word-of-mouth recommendations are extremely powerful, and providing incentives can encourage consumers to share their excellent experiences with others, therefore extending your client base.

Attend industry events, trade exhibitions, or conferences to promote your products or services. Build relationships and create leads through networking with potential consumers, industry leaders, and partners. Take advantage of these events to display your knowledge and interact with prospects in person.

Personalize your marketing efforts to provide potential clients with a customized experience. Make use of client data and segmentation strategies to send personalized messages and offers based on their interests and preferences. To leave a lasting impression, use tailored email marketing, retargeting advertisements, or customized landing sites.

To persuade new consumers to try your products or services, offer incentives or promotions. To generate a feeling of urgency and promote action, consider offering limited-time discounts, free trials, or exclusive deals. Highlight the distinct value customers will obtain by selecting your brand over rivals.

Monitor and analyze your marketing activities to see which techniques work best in recruiting new consumers. Keep track of important data like website traffic, conversion rates, lead creation, and customer acquisition expenses. Use this information to fine-tune your marketing plans and campaigns for better outcomes.

Remember that recruiting new clients is a continuous activity. Adapt and fine-tune your marketing strategy in response to client input, industry developments, and emerging technology. Maintain awareness of your target audience's shifting requirements and preferences to ensure that your marketing activities stay relevant and successful.

Building Customer Loyalty

Customer loyalty is similar to developing a long-term relationship built on trust, fulfillment, and emotional connection. It entails providing consistently outstanding experiences, exceeding expectations, and cultivating a sense of loyalty and advocacy within your consumer base. Let's take a slow and easy approach to this concept:

Consumer loyalty is earned through meeting and surpassing consumer expectations on a continual basis. Begin by learning about your consumers' wants, desires, and preferences. Gather feedback on a regular basis via surveys, reviews, and consumer contacts to acquire insights into their experiences and expectations.

At every touchpoint, provide great customer service. Train and empower your workers to go above and above when it comes to responding to customer questions, quickly resolving issues, and establishing memorable experiences. A great customer service experience may create an indelible impression and help to the development of loyalty.

Concentrate on providing high-quality products or services that meet or exceed client expectations on a constant basis. Strive for perfection in all aspects of your offerings, from design to usefulness to performance and longevity. To stay ahead of the competition and deliver value that keeps consumers coming back, you must constantly innovate and develop.

Create emotional relationships with your consumers by learning about their beliefs, goals, and pain spots. Create brand messaging and marketing that speaks to their emotions and gives them a sense of belonging. Empathize with consumers, personalize conversations, and make them feel appreciated and understood.

In order to reward and incentive repeat purchases and consumer advocacy, implement a loyalty program. Show your thanks for their loyalty by providing unique discounts, special promotions, or access to VIP advantages. A well-designed loyalty program may instill a sense of exclusivity and belonging in your consumer base.

Engage with your clients on a regular basis using multiple channels such as social media, email newsletters, and community forums. To stay top of mind and demonstrate your dedication to their success, provide excellent information, industry insights, and tailored recommendations. Encourage two-way communication to strengthen connections and develop a feeling of community.

Surprise and thrill your customers with unexpected expressions of gratitude. Personalized thank-you messages, birthday or anniversary presents, or special previews of new items are examples of this. These tiny gestures can help to create memorable encounters and strengthen your emotional connection with your brand.

In order to track and evaluate consumer interactions and preferences, invest in customer relationship management (CRM) technologies. Make use of data to customize your marketing efforts and match your services to the demands of specific customers. Use the knowledge obtained to predict their future requirements and offer proactive solutions.

Encourage and swiftly reply to client comments. Actively listen to their opinions, complaints, and improvement ideas. Show that you appreciate their ideas and take their feedback seriously. You demonstrate your commitment to continual improvement by implementing their input into your goods, services, and procedures.

By connecting consumers, you can foster a feeling of community. Allow consumers to share their experiences, discuss ideas, and offer assistance to one another. This can be accomplished through the use of online forums, user groups, or consumer events. Building a community builds loyalty and develops a sense of belonging.

Remember that developing client loyalty is an ongoing process. Consistency, honesty, and a real dedication to surpassing client expectations are required. You can establish a loyal client base that not only returns but also becomes brand advocates, recommending your business to others, by providing extraordinary experiences, building emotional connections, and rewarding loyalty.

Enhancing the Customer Experience

Improving the customer experience is like sprinkling some fairy dust on every encounter your customers have with your company. Understanding their journey, anticipating their requirements, and going above and beyond to create memorable and good experiences are all part of it. Let's take a slow and easy approach to this concept:

Begin by outlining the client path, from initial contact through post-purchase contacts. Identify touchpoints and opportunities to improve the experience. contacts across numerous channels such as your website, social media, customer service, and in-person contacts are all included.

Personalize the experience by learning about your consumers' preferences and customizing interactions to their needs. Offer tailored suggestions, relevant information, and targeted offers based on consumer data and insights. Make each customer feel appreciated and understood by treating them as individuals.

Remove friction points and obstructions to simplify and streamline the client journey. Optimize your website and user interface to provide a consistent and easy-to-use experience. Provide clear and straightforward information, reduce checkout stages, and provide self-service solutions for typical queries.

Train and empower your personnel to provide outstanding customer service. Provide them with the information and resources they need to successfully and efficiently answer consumer demands. To establish a good and helpful environment for customers, encourage empathy, active listening, and problem-solving abilities.

Maintain consistency across all mediums and touchpoints. Check to see whether your brand message, tone of voice, and visual identity are consistent throughout your website, social media, emails, and in-person contacts. Customers will feel more connected to your brand if you maintain consistency.

Anticipate and surpass customers' expectations. Proactively assist clients by delivering pertinent information, anticipating questions, and providing answers before they ask. Surprise and thrill them with out-of-the-ordinary gestures, tailored suggestions, or special deals that exceed their expectations.

Seek feedback from customers and actively listen to their comments and problems. Allow consumers to share their experiences through different channels, such as surveys, reviews, or social media. Use this feedback to find areas for improvement and make the required changes to improve the customer experience.

Wherever possible, incorporate technology and automation to increase efficiency and convenience. Implement chatbots or AI-powered customer care solutions to deliver rapid replies and help 24 hours a day, seven days a week. Data analytics may help you obtain insights into consumer behavior and preferences, allowing you to customise experiences and create data-driven enhancements.

Create a customer-focused culture within your company. Encourage all workers to take ownership of providing outstanding service by cultivating a mentality that values the client experience. Instill a sense of pride and purpose in surpassing customer expectations, and recognize and reward workers that go above and beyond to improve the customer experience.

To keep ahead of client expectations, you must constantly innovate and grow. Maintain an awareness of industry trends, developing technology, and client preferences. To surprise and please your consumers, try out new products, services, or engagement techniques. Adopt a culture of continuous improvement and look for methods to improve the customer experience on a regular basis.

Remember that improving the customer experience is a continual process. It necessitates a thorough awareness of your consumers, a dedication to provide outstanding service, and a drive to always improve. You can establish a customer-centric culture that distinguishes your business and encourages long-term loyalty by offering personalized experiences, streamlining procedures, and surpassing expectations.

Implementing Customer Relationship Management (CRM) Systems

Implementing customer relationship management (CRM) solutions is similar to having a trustworthy assistant that assists you in developing strong and long-lasting ties with your clients. It entails leveraging technology and data to manage customer interactions, track vital data, and enhance sales and marketing operations. Let's take a slow and easy approach to this concept:

A CRM system is an effective tool for centralizing customer data, streamlining operations, and improving overall customer relationship management. It enables organizations to collect and manage consumer data such as contact information, purchase history, preferences, and communication records.

You may better understand your clients and their demands by establishing a CRM system. It allows you to develop detailed client profiles, segment your consumer base, and learn about their interests and activities. This data-driven strategy allows you to more effectively personalize your services and marketing messages to specific client categories.

CRM solutions make internal communication and cooperation more efficient. They offer a consolidated platform via which sales, marketing, and customer support teams may access and update client information in real time. This allows for smooth transitions across departments, provides consistent message, and improves the overall customer experience.

You may save time and increase productivity by automating common operations and workflows using a CRM system. This includes email marketing campaigns, lead nurturing procedures, and follow-up actions that are automated. Your staff may focus on more value-added activities and creating deeper client connections by automating routine operations.

CRM systems give useful information about sales and marketing performance. They create statistics and analytics to assist you in assessing the efficacy of your campaigns, tracking sales KPIs, and identifying areas for improvement. This data-driven strategy enables you to make educated decisions, optimize your tactics, and increase income.

Putting in place a CRM system increases customer service and support. Your staff can give tailored and quick help to customers if they have access to detailed customer information. They can immediately review purchase history, respond to enquiries or difficulties, and provide customised solutions. This improves the consumer experience and increases loyalty.

CRM systems provide for customized marketing initiatives as well as lead management. You may provide targeted marketing messages, offers, and suggestions to particular consumer segments by exploiting customer data and segmentation capabilities. This tailored strategy improves conversion rates and promotes client engagement.

CRM solutions improve relationship building and client retention by centralizing customer data and interactions. They provide proactive relationship management by sending reminders and alerts for follow-ups, contract renewals, and upsell possibilities. This allows you to maintain contact with consumers and cultivate long-term partnerships.

CRM systems also aid in forecasting and the management of sales pipelines. They make sales prospects visible, track deal progress, and anticipate income. This allows for more efficient resource allocation, more accurate sales forecasting, and better decision-making to support corporate success.

It is critical to maintain sufficient data security and privacy protections while adopting a CRM system. Protect client information and follow data protection standards. To retain trust and secrecy, train your staff on correct data management and promote adherence to privacy regulations.

Implementing a CRM system provides various advantages to firms, including greater customer understanding, simpler procedures, increased productivity, targeted marketing, and stronger customer connections. You can optimize your sales and marketing operations, generate growth, and provide excellent customer experiences by employing technology to manage and analyze customer data.

Chapter 10: Innovation and Continuous Improvement

Fostering a Culture of Innovation

Fostering an innovation culture is similar to establishing an atmosphere in which ideas are nourished, creativity is encouraged, and everyone feels empowered to contribute to the organization's growth and success. It entails accepting change, creating a continuous improvement attitude, and giving the necessary support and resources to develop innovative thinking. Let's take a slow and easy approach to this concept:

Creating an innovative culture begins with leadership that celebrates and supports innovation. Leaders must establish a clear vision and explain the value of innovation throughout the business. They should promote risk-taking, reward innovation, and set a good example by being open to new ideas and embracing change.

Encourage open and inclusive communication channels that foster cooperation and the exchange of ideas. Create an environment in which everyone, regardless of function or level within the business, feels comfortable expressing their views and opinions. Encourage cross-functional cooperation and provide chances for idea generation and exchange.

Encourage inquiry and a lifelong learning mentality. Instill the importance of obtaining new knowledge, exploring fresh viewpoints, and remaining current on industry trends and developing technology. Encourage staff to participate in professional development programs, conferences, and innovation-focused projects.

Provide the resources and support needed for innovation. This entails committing time, money, and people to specific innovation initiatives. Create innovation laboratories or designated areas for employees to explore, develop, and test new ideas. Create a culture that values failure as a vital stepping stone toward innovation and development.

Recognize and appreciate creativity and ingenuity. Individuals or teams who produce creative ideas or contribute to the effective execution of successful innovations should be recognized and rewarded. This can involve public acclaim, prizes, or opportunity for progress in one's job. Celebrating accomplishments emphasizes the value of creativity and encourages others to submit their ideas.

Accept an experimental and iterative mentality. Employees should be encouraged to test theories, launch new projects, and learn from feedback. Create a safe workplace in which measured risks are encouraged and failure is viewed as a great learning opportunity. Encourage a readiness to pivot and change based on experimentation insights.

Break down silos and promote idea cross-pollination. Make it possible for employees from other departments or teams to cooperate and share their experience. Encourage the mixing of diverse ideas to foster creativity by cultivating a culture that appreciates variety of opinion.

Create methods and systems that encourage creativity. Idea management systems, innovation challenges, and hackathons are examples of this. Encourage workers to capture and share their ideas, to give feedback, and to work together to refine and develop concepts. This systematic technique aids in the successful collection, evaluation, and implementation of new ideas.

Provide chances for training and growth in the areas of innovation and creative thinking. Provide workshops, classes, or mentorship programs to workers to help them strengthen their innovative abilities, such as design thinking or problem-solving strategies. This investment in talent development increases the organization's overall innovative capabilities.

Assess and monitor innovation activities on a regular basis. Create key performance indicators (KPIs) to measure metrics linked to innovation, such as the number of ideas developed, successful implementations, or the effect of innovations on business results. Review and evaluate these indicators on a regular basis to find areas for improvement and to fine-tune innovation plans.

Remember that cultivating an innovative culture needs a long-term commitment and ongoing work. It entails fostering an environment that encourages creativity, cooperation, and the discovery of novel ideas. You can develop a culture that fosters continuous improvement, maintains your business adaptive, and places you at the forefront of your industry by embracing innovation, giving resources and assistance, and recognizing and rewarding innovative ideas.

Encouraging Creative Problem-Solving

Encouraging creative problem-solving is like releasing your team's latent ability to develop inventive and effective solutions to problems. It entails creating a supportive atmosphere in which people feel encouraged to think outside the box, challenge conventional ways, and apply their unique views and abilities to tackle challenging challenges. Let's take a slow and easy approach to this concept:

Create a non-judgmental environment in which people feel comfortable expressing their ideas and beliefs. Create a culture that supports and accepts different points of view and fosters open-mindedness. Create a collaborative setting that promotes active listening, constructive criticism, and the exploration of alternative problem-solving strategies.

Encourage curiosity and a mentality of constant learning. Encourage a culture of questioning, seeking new information, and challenging preconceptions. Encourage individuals to broaden their problem-solving toolset by exploring other disciplines, industries, and sources of inspiration.

Opportunities for professional growth and skill-building in areas such as critical thinking, creative problem-solving strategies, and innovative processes should be made available. Provide training programs, workshops, or mentorship efforts that improve people's problem-solving talents and encourage the use of innovative ideas.

Adopt an experimental and failure-learning mentality. Encourage people to take measured risks and look for unusual solutions. Create an environment in which failure is viewed as a source of growth and learning rather than a setback. Encourage people to reflect on their mistakes, glean useful insights, and apply what they've learned to future problem-solving initiatives.

Individuals should be given the opportunity to take ownership of problem-solving projects. Allow individuals to explore and develop their ideas by giving them autonomy and decision-making authority when appropriate. Encourage them to take the initiative, be resourceful, and look for chances to solve problems on their own or in cross-functional teams.

Encourage multidisciplinary cooperation by developing platforms or projects that bring people from various backgrounds and areas of expertise together. Create a culture that promotes the interchange of ideas, stimulates group problem solving, and recognizes the worth of various viewpoints. To foster creative problem-solving, set aside time for brainstorming, collaborative workshops, or design thinking sessions.

Recognize and reward innovative problem-solving approaches. Celebrate and showcase successful problem-solving activities, highlighting individuals or teams that have shown innovative thinking and generated meaningful results. To inspire and encourage individuals to engage in innovative problem-solving, provide incentives like as recognition, bonuses, or prospects for progress in their careers.

Encourage the use of visualization tools such as mind mapping or drawing to help with idea development and issue solving. Encourage others to think visually by representing issues and potential answers with diagrams, charts, or visual metaphors. Visual representations can assist people in thinking more creatively and identifying new connections between concepts.

Create online and physical venues for idea exchange and cooperation. To support distant working and idea sharing, use collaboration solutions such as project management software or virtual collaboration platforms. In order to motivate and drive creative problem-solving across the business, cultivate a culture of sharing best practices, success stories, and lessons learned.

Allow folks time and space to participate in unstructured thought and introspection. Encourage individuals to take pauses, downtime, or allocated "innovation time" to step away from their regular obligations and allow their brains to roam, fostering fresh views and breakthrough ideas.

Remember that supporting creative problem-solving is a continual process that involves continuing support, open communication, and a loving atmosphere. You can unleash your team's full creative potential and drive significant solutions to complicated issues by cultivating a culture that promotes curiosity, experimentation, cooperation, and rewards new ideas.

Embracing Lean and Agile Methodologies

Adopting lean and agile approaches is the equivalent of taking a flexible and iterative approach to project management and process improvement. It entails accepting change, promoting teamwork, and consistently providing value to customers. Let's take a slow and easy approach to this concept:

By concentrating on client demands and reacting to changing conditions, lean and agile techniques attempt to optimize efficiency and value. They place an emphasis on providing tiny, incremental changes and products while encouraging cooperation, transparency, and continual learning.

Lean technique stresses waste minimization and process improvement. Identifying and removing non-value-added operations, decreasing redundant procedures, and optimizing workflows are all part of the process. Organizations may maximize resources, cut costs, and increase overall efficiency by reducing waste.

Agile approach, on the other hand, encourages project management flexibility and adaptation. It entails breaking down tasks into smaller, more manageable chunks known as "sprints" or "iterations." Teams collaborate to deliver and iterate on work while adjusting to changing needs and feedback.

Organizations can get various advantages by implementing lean and agile approaches. They are able to react swiftly to market changes, client needs, and new possibilities. This enables speedier innovation, shorter time to market, and a competitive advantage in dynamically changing sectors.

These approaches encourage a collaborative atmosphere and enable teams to make choices collaboratively. They promote cross-functional collaboration and open communication to ensure goal alignment and shared ownership. This fosters team members' sense of responsibility, accountability, and involvement.

Customer value is prioritized in lean and agile processes by concentrating on providing the most critical features and upgrades first. This customer-centric strategy assists firms in meeting customer demands more successfully by allocating resources to areas that have the most impact.

These techniques also encourage ongoing development through feedback loops and retrospectives on a regular basis. Organizations may continually improve their practices and performance by encouraging teams to reflect on their work, identify areas for development, and adapt their processes and methods appropriately.

To effectively implement lean and agile approaches, firms must foster a climate that encourages experimentation, learning, and risk-taking. They must equip teams with the tools, training, and resources they need to adopt these techniques and change their work processes accordingly.

To enhance openness, cooperation, and alignment, organizations should also develop clear communication channels, such as daily stand-up meetings or agile boards. This allows teams to stay focused, assess progress, and handle any difficulties or roadblocks as they arise.

Furthermore, adopting lean and agile approaches necessitates that firms adopt a philosophy of continual learning and growth. It entails accepting both internal and external feedback and using it as a driver for growth and adaptation. Organizations must foster an experimental culture and enable teams to take measured risks in the quest of innovation and efficiency.

In conclusion, adopting lean and agile approaches allows firms to become more adaptive, customer-focused, and efficient. Organizations may adapt to changing market dynamics and consumer needs with agility and resilience by cutting waste, encouraging cooperation, and consistently providing value. This strategy empowers employees, encourages creativity, and allows firms to stay ahead in today's fast-paced and competitive corporate environment.

Implementing Continuous Improvement Processes

Implementing continuous improvement methods is akin to laying the groundwork for an organization's continued development and progress. It entails developing a systematic process to identifying areas for improvement, implementing changes, and tracking results. Organizations may improve efficiency, quality, and overall performance by cultivating a culture of continual learning and improvement. Let's take a slow and easy approach to this concept:

Continuous improvement is all about striving for excellence and finding incremental methods to improve many parts of a company. It all starts with developing a mentality that accepts change and encourages people at all levels to look for ways to improve.

Begin by building a continuous improvement framework, such as the Plan-Do-Check-Act (PDCA) cycle or the Lean Six Sigma technique. These approaches give a systematic approach to identifying possibilities for improvement, implementing changes, measuring results, and iterating for further improvement.

Encourage staff to actively participate in the process of continuous improvement. Create a climate in which everyone feels comfortable sharing ideas, thoughts, and improvements. Encourage cross-functional cooperation since different points of view typically result in more thorough and inventive solutions.

Assess and evaluate processes, workflows, and outcomes on a regular basis to discover opportunities for improvement. Conducting process audits, obtaining input from customers and staff, and employing data-driven insights to uncover bottlenecks, inefficiencies, or quality concerns are all examples of this.

Prioritize possibilities for improvement based on their potential effect and feasibility. Concentrate on activities that are in line with company objectives, client demands, or key performance metrics. This helps to guarantee that resources are used wisely and that improvements provide significant effects.

Before implementing changes on a large scale, use an organized strategy, such as pilot projects or small-scale experiments. This enables the assessment of possible hazards and the improvement of solutions based on feedback and lessons gained.

Gradual adoption minimizes interruptions and allows for modifications along the way.

Encourage a culture of failure learning and success celebration. Highlight the significance of testing, while understanding that not all attempts will provide the intended results. Encourage people and teams to see setbacks as opportunities for growth and to learn from them in order to strengthen future efforts.

Provide staff with training and resources to assist them in their attempts to develop continuously. Provide problem-solving workshops, seminars, or online courses that focus on process mapping, data analysis, and other applicable skills. Employees are empowered to actively contribute to continuous improvement efforts when they are given the required tools and expertise.

Create systems for capturing and sharing excellent practices and lessons learned. Encourage workers to document their attempts to improve and to share their findings with others in the organization. This encourages information exchange and aids in the spread of good practices throughout the business.

Evaluate and monitor the effect of improvement activities on a regular basis. To assess the success of implemented improvements, track key performance indicators like as efficiency measures, customer satisfaction ratings, or defect rates. This allows firms to quantify the advantages of continuous improvement activities and highlight areas that need more attention.

Individuals and teams should be celebrated and recognized for their contributions to continual development. Highlight success stories, discuss outcomes, and recognize those who have made a major contribution. This emphasizes the need of ongoing development and encourages others to participate actively in the process.

Remember that establishing continuous improvement procedures is a constant journey that needs dedication and a growth mentality. Organizations can continually improve their operations, boost efficiency, and remain competitive in an ever-changing business market by cultivating a culture that accepts change, supports learning, and rewards innovation.

Chapter 11: Expanding into New Markets

Market Expansion Strategies

Market expansion strategies are company tactics and actions used to enter new markets or extend their position in existing ones. These tactics are designed to capitalize on chances for expansion, reach new clients, and optimize income potential. Let's take a slow and easy approach to this concept:

Geographical expansion is one market growth technique in which enterprises penetrate new geographical regions or nations. This may entail opening additional branches, businesses, or offices in various areas. Businesses may tap into untapped client populations, get access to new distribution channels, and diversify their income sources by expanding into new areas.

Product diversification is another approach in which firms add new items or services to their existing consumer base or target new customer categories. This strategy enables businesses to provide a greater range of products by using existing brand name, customer relationships, and distribution networks. Businesses may react to changing client demands and tastes, improve market share, and develop new revenue sources by diversifying their product line.

Market penetration is a method for growing market share in current markets. To attract more consumers, increase marketing and sales activities, extend distribution channels, or provide competitive pricing. Market penetration strategies seek to increase market share by outperforming competitors or gaining consumer loyalty.

Targeting new consumer groups inside current markets is part of a market development strategy. This may be accomplished by tailoring products or services to the individual requirements and preferences of various consumer groups. Businesses may extend their client base and improve revenue without entering new markets by discovering and entering new consumer niches.

Another market expansion approach is strategic alliances and collaborations. Companies can use each other's resources, knowledge, and client bases by partnering with other firms, whether through joint ventures, alliances, or strategic partnerships. These agreements allow organizations to enter new markets or reach out to new client groups in a more efficient and effective manner.

Acquisitions and mergers are market growth methods in which corporations purchase or combine with other organizations in order to obtain access to new markets, consumers, technology, or skills. Companies can use this method to swiftly grow their market presence and solidify their position within an industry. Acquisitions and mergers can result in cost savings, greater market share, and increased competitiveness.

E-commerce and digital growth plans entail using online platforms and technology to reach out to new customers and extend market reach. Establishing an online presence, utilizing social media and digital marketing channels, or collaborating with e-commerce platforms are all examples of this. Businesses may use e-commerce techniques to transcend regional limits, target worldwide consumers, and profit on the expanding trend of online buying.

Another technique for market expansion is to enter new market categories or niches. This entails discovering underdeveloped or untapped market groups and adapting products or services to suit unique need. Businesses may differentiate themselves from competition and acquire a niche market, which may bring untapped development prospects, by delivering specialized solutions.

Before adopting any market development plan, it is critical to undertake extensive market research and analysis. This assists firms in comprehending market dynamics, client preferences, the competitive environment, and regulatory needs. A well-informed strategy ensures that resources are properly allocated, risks are reduced, and the technique adopted is aligned with the overall corporate objectives.

Overall, market expansion tactics enable organizations to develop, gain market share, and capitalize on new income sources. Businesses can position themselves for long-term success and sustainable development in an ever-changing business landscape by proactively entering new markets, expanding services, targeting various client segments, or forging strategic partnerships.

Assessing Market Potential and Entry Barriers

Evaluating the attractiveness and feasibility of joining a certain market is part of assessing market potential and entry barriers. It necessitates an examination of market dynamics, client demand, rivalry, and the obstacles to market entry. Let's take a slow and easy approach to this concept:

Understanding the size and development possibilities of a target market is required for market potential evaluation. This includes looking at things like population demographics, economic data, industry trends, and consumer behavior. Businesses may identify the income opportunity and development potential of a certain market by examining market potential.

Analyzing customer demand is critical for determining market potential. It entails determining the demands, interests, and purchasing habits of the market's target customers. Businesses may win a considerable market share by understanding client demand and aligning their products or services to respond to specific customer demands.

Analyzing competition is critical for determining market potential. It entails assessing the competitive landscape, which includes current competitors, market share, strengths, weaknesses, and market positioning. Competition analysis assists firms in understanding the degree of competition they may encounter and identifying chances to differentiate themselves and obtain a competitive edge.

Evaluating entrance barriers is an important part of determining market potential. Entry barriers are impediments or limitations to a company's entry into a market. Regulatory constraints, large financial investments, intellectual property protection, distribution networks, established brand loyalty, and technological difficulties are examples of these impediments. Understanding entrance barriers enables organizations to anticipate and handle potential problems during market entry.

Market research and analysis are essential in determining market potential and entry obstacles. It entails gathering relevant facts and insights about the target market through primary and secondary research. Surveys, interviews, or focus groups with potential consumers are examples of primary research, whereas secondary research include examining current market data, reports, and industry studies.

Analyzing market trends and projections is a necessary step in determining market potential. It entails investigating industry data, economic indicators, consumer trends, and technology advances that may have an influence on the market's future growth and attractiveness. Businesses may detect new possibilities and make educated market entrance decisions by staying current on market trends.

Regulatory and legal aspects are critical in determining market potential. Businesses must comprehend the target market's legal requirements, trade rules, licenses, permits, and compliance standards. Failure to adequately manage the regulatory framework can create major hurdles to market entrance.

In order to determine market potential, infrastructural and logistical issues must be evaluated. It entails determining the availability and quality of transportation networks, communication infrastructure, supply chain capabilities, and other resources needed to operate successfully in the target market. Infrastructure constraints may either offer obstacles or generate possibilities depending on the needs of the organization.

A thorough and holistic strategy is required to assess market potential and entry constraints. It entails the integration of qualitative and quantitative data, market research, competitive analysis, and industry knowledge. Businesses may make educated judgments regarding market entrance, identify possible risks and opportunities, and establish effective strategies to overcome hurdles and thrive in the target market by performing a complete evaluation.

Remember that determining market potential and entry obstacles is a continuous process. Market dynamics can shift over time, bringing with them new difficulties and possibilities. Continuous monitoring of market trends, consumer preferences, regulatory changes, and the competitive landscape assists firms in adapting their strategies and making educated decisions in order to optimize their chances of success in the target market.

Developing Market Entry Strategies

Creating market entrance strategies include creating plans and activities to enter a new market or grow one's position in an existing market. Understanding the target market, identifying opportunities, mitigating risks, and executing effective market entrance techniques all require a methodical approach. Let's take a slow and easy approach to this concept:

The cornerstone of designing market entrance strategy is market research and analysis. It entails collecting and analyzing pertinent data on the target market, such as customer demographics, purchasing habits, market size, competition, regulatory environment, and cultural subtleties. This data gives useful insights to help drive decision-making and strategy creation.

Targeting and segmentation are critical aspects in creating market entrance strategies. Businesses may adjust their services to match the distinct requirements and preferences of certain client groups by recognizing them within the market. This aids in optimizing marketing efforts and efficiently allocating resources to grab the most attractive possibilities.

Choosing the best means of market entry is a vital choice. It entails deciding on the best way to enter the market, such as exporting, licensing, franchising, strategic alliances, joint ventures, or establishing a subsidiary. Each option has advantages and disadvantages based on market circumstances, resource availability, and risk tolerance.

It is critical to create a value proposition that connects with the target market. It entails establishing and articulating the distinct benefits and value that a company provides to its clients. A compelling value proposition distinguishes the company from rivals and attracts the attention of the target market, eventually influencing their purchase decisions.

Market entrance plans must include pricing and distribution strategies. Pricing strategies that are ideal take into account elements such as client affordability, competition, and cost structures. Distribution plans entail determining the most effective means for reaching the target market, as well as guaranteeing efficient product availability and client access.

Promotional and marketing methods are essential for market access. This involves creating a detailed marketing plan including the strategies for increasing awareness, generating interest, and driving customer acquisition. Advertising, public relations, digital marketing, social media campaigns, and targeted promotional activities are all possible components of the plans.

Creating alliances and relationships inside the target market might help you enter the market successfully. Collaboration with local distributors, suppliers, influencers, or industry groups may give significant market insights, make distribution routes more accessible, and increase credibility and confidence among local customers.

Adapting products or services to meet the demands and preferences of the target market is sometimes required for effective market entrance. This may entail adaptation, localization, or even invention to ensure that the products correspond with the target market's cultural, regulatory, and competitive situation. Understanding and responding to client expectations and preferences is critical for market adoption.

In creating market entrance strategy, risk assessment and mitigation measures are critical. Businesses must identify and assess possible risks such as political insecurity, legal obstacles, economic volatility, and competitive hurdles. Creating contingency planning and risk mitigation techniques assists organizations in navigating uncertainty and mitigating potential negative effects on market entrance initiatives.

Throughout the market entrance process, continuous monitoring and assessment are required. Assessing the efficacy of market entrance tactics on a regular basis enables firms to track progress, make appropriate modifications, and refine their strategy based on market feedback and changing dynamics.

Remember that building market entrance strategy needs thorough research, preparation, and flexibility. Understanding the target market, aligning offers with consumer wants, and implementing successful marketing and distribution strategies are all critical. Businesses may boost their chances of success and establish a solid footing in new markets or expand their presence in current areas by adopting a well-rounded market entrance plan.

Adapting Products and Services to New Markets

Adapting products and services to new markets is the process of changing existing offers to meet the demands, preferences, and cultural subtleties of a new target market. It entails customizing products and services to the specific features of the new market in order to boost their relevance and attractiveness. Let's take a slow and easy approach to this concept:

The first step in modifying products and services is to understand the target market. This entails undertaking extensive market research to learn about client demographics, behaviors, purchasing patterns, and cultural aspects. Businesses may find opportunities for improvement by knowing their target market's preferences and expectations.

Determine the important aspects or attributes of present products or services that require modification. This might include assessing things including functioning, design, packaging, branding, price, and customer service. Prioritizing the changes based on their potential impact and relevance to the target market is critical.

Localization is a typical method of adaptation. It entails tailoring the product or service to the new market's linguistic, cultural, and regulatory needs. This includes translating product labels, packaging, marketing materials, and even changing product names to appeal to local consumers.

Adapting to new markets may also entail changing the features, specs, or functionality of a product or service to fit with local client preferences. This might include adopting certain design aspects, adding or eliminating features, or changing the product's size or format to better meet the demands of the target market.

Another key part of modifying products and services is pricing. Consider the affordability, purchasing power, and price sensitivity of the target market. Adapting pricing strategies to reflect local market conditions aids in ensuring that offers are competitive and appealing to target customers.

To guarantee effective delivery of products or services to the new market, distribution and logistics may need to be modified. This might include building local alliances, utilizing local distribution networks, or changing the supply chain to fit the target market's particular requirements and infrastructure.

Customer service and after-sales assistance may also need customization. Localized customer support, warranty services, and maintenance programs may improve the entire customer experience and foster confidence and loyalty in the new market.

During the adaption phase, feedback and market testing are critical. Gathering feedback from potential clients or doing market testing enables organizations to validate the efficacy of their modifications and make any required changes. This iterative method allows the product or service to be fine-tuned to fit the unique demands of the target market.

Working with local partners, consultants, or advisers can give useful insights and direction throughout the adaptation process. Their knowledge and experience of the local market may assist in identifying areas that require adaptation and ensuring that changes are culturally suitable and in line with market expectations.

It is critical to monitor and evaluate the performance of modified goods and services. Data collection on sales, customer feedback, and market response allows organizations to evaluate the success of the modifications and make data-driven choices on additional improvements or changes.

Product and service adaptation to new markets is a dynamic and iterative process. Continuous learning, adaptability, and a thorough grasp of the target market are all required. Businesses may boost their chances of success, acquire a competitive edge, and create strong customer connections in the new market by adapting offerings to the particular demands and preferences of the new market.

Chapter 12: Building Strategic Partnerships and Alliances

Identifying Strategic Partnership Opportunities

Identifying strategic partnership possibilities entails identifying and analyzing prospective collaborations with other companies in order to accomplish mutual goals and advantages. It is a proactive strategy to using external resources, talents, and experience to improve competitive advantage and promote development. Let's take a slow and easy approach to this concept:

Understanding the organization's aims and objectives is the first step in identifying strategic cooperation prospects. It entails determining where collaboration with external partners might provide value, such as extending market reach, gaining access to new technology, sharing expenses, or entering new markets.

Market research and analysis are critical in locating possible partners. Organizations can find firms or entities that complement their strengths, fill gaps in their services, or share comparable target markets by examining the competitive environment, client needs, and industry trends.

Consider forming alliances with firms that provide complementary products or services. This enables companies to provide a more comprehensive service to clients, resulting in a win-win situation for both sides. Organizations may improve their value proposition and differentiate themselves in the market by combining skills and resources.

Determine suitable collaborators based on their knowledge and capabilities. Look for firms with specialized expertise, technology, or one-of-a-kind assets that connect with your strategic goals. To achieve a solid relationship match, evaluate their track record, reputation, and consistency with your organization's beliefs and culture.

Think about forming strategic partnerships with rivals or groups in related industry. Collaboration with competitors may result in synergies, the pooling of resources, and the acceleration of innovation. Partnerships with complementary sectors can open up new market prospects and enable firms to reach new client groups.

Networking and business events are excellent places to meet possible partners. Attend conferences, trade exhibitions, or industry-specific events to network with other companies and seek cooperation opportunities. Engage in discussions, exchange thoughts, and cultivate relationships that may lead to beneficial collaborations.

Potential collaborators include government agencies, research institutes, and educational institutions. These organizations frequently have substantial resources, research capabilities, and networks that may help with innovation, product development, or market growth. Investigate options for public-private partnerships or research collaborations that will allow them to harness their knowledge and resources.

Participate in open innovation efforts and investigate startup ecosystems. Startups frequently have disruptive technology or novel viewpoints that can fuel innovation and market upheaval. Organizations may tap into the agility, inventiveness, and entrepreneurial spirit of startups by forming relationships with them.

Create a strategic partnership structure outlining each partner's objectives, expectations, and duties. Establish clear communication routes, governance frameworks, and decision-making and conflict-resolution methods. Building trust and maintaining open channels of communication are essential for successful collaboration.

Assess and evaluate the success of strategic alliances on a regular basis. To assess the efficacy of the relationship, track key performance measures such as customer happiness, revenue growth, and innovation outputs. Review the partnership's alignment with corporate goals on a regular basis and alter the plan as appropriate.

Keep in mind that spotting strategic collaboration possibilities necessitates a proactive and strategic approach. It entails thinking about the organization's goals, researching the market, and looking for firms with complementary resources and talents. Organizations may use common strengths, generate innovation, and uncover new development prospects by building strategic alliances in a collaborative and mutually beneficial manner.

Collaborating with Industry Leaders

Collaborating with industry leaders entails forming alliances or collaborations with notable and powerful organizations within a certain sector. This strategic strategy seeks to capitalize on industry leaders' experience, reputation, and market position in order to create mutual advantages and accelerate corporate success. Let's take a slow and easy approach to this concept:

Collaboration with industry leaders provides several benefits to companies. Organizations may benefit from the considerable industry expertise, best practices, and networks of well-established and reputable enterprises by cooperating with them. This relationship gives firms access to vital insights, market information, and industry trends, allowing them to stay on the cutting edge of innovation and remain competitive.

Industry leaders frequently have a large consumer base and a well-known brand. Collaboration with them enables firms to capitalize on their reputation and credibility, which may boost their own brand image and market placement. This affiliation with industry experts may develop client trust and confidence, resulting in enhanced credibility and additional commercial prospects.

Collaboration with industry experts opens access to new markets and commercial prospects. businesses can acquire access to new clients, distribution channels, and market segments that were previously out of reach by partnering with businesses that have a significant market presence. This broadens their reach and has the potential to lead to tremendous development and expansion.

Collaboration with industry experts promotes information exchange and learning. Organizations may exchange ideas, knowledge, and insights through cooperation. This knowledge exchange allows both sides to learn from one another, adapt best practices, and explore new growth and innovation methods. It promotes an industry-wide culture of continual learning and development.

Working with industry leaders can help to speed up innovation and product development. Organizations can join forces to combine their resources, research skills, and technological experience in order to produce cutting-edge goods or services. This collaboration frequently results in the development of novel solutions that fulfill market demands more effectively and efficiently.

Partnerships with industry leaders can provide access to pooled resources and scale economies. Collaboration can result in cost savings, shared purchasing power, and shared infrastructure. Organizations may use this to maximize resource use, cut costs, and increase operational efficiency.

Collaboration with industry experts allows for networking and the expansion of professional relationships. It enables businesses to engage with important individuals, essential stakeholders, and other industry participants. Building ties with industry experts may lead to new business collaborations, strategic alliances, and possible investors.

Collaboration with industry leaders involves clear communication, mutual trust, and goal alignment. Transparent governance systems, clearly defined responsibilities, and a common goal are critical. Regular communication and collaboration serve to keep the relationship productive and guarantee that both sides get the most out of the collaboration.

It is critical to evaluate the collaboration's outcomes and effect on a regular basis. Monitoring important performance measures, like as revenue growth, customer happiness, or market share, aids in assessing the collaboration's efficacy. This enables firms to make changes and tweaks as needed to guarantee the collaboration continues to provide value.

In summary, cooperating with industry experts delivers various benefits to firms, including access to knowledge, market opportunities, resources, and shared learning. Organizations may improve their competitive position, stimulate innovation, and open up new growth opportunities by forging strategic partnerships with industry leaders. These collaborations build a collaborative culture and help firms to succeed in a dynamic and competitive commercial world.

Leveraging Alliances for Growth

Leveraging alliances for growth entails leveraging the power of strategic partnerships and alliances to promote corporate expansion, boost market share, and open new doors. This technique enables enterprises to leverage the capabilities and resources of their alliance partners in order to achieve common goals and accelerate growth. Let's take a slow and easy approach to this concept:

Joint ventures, collaborations, consortiums, and strategic partnerships are all examples of alliances. They bring firms with complementary talents, resources, or market access together to produce synergies and mutual growth. Organizations can achieve more by combining their talents than they could separately.

Alliances enable firms to get access to new markets and client groups. firms can extend their reach and penetrate new geographical regions or client groups by collaborating with firms that have existing market presence or access to unexplored markets. This simplifies market access and lowers the obstacles to entering new markets on one's own.

Alliances allow firms to share the risks and expenses of corporate development. Organizations that collaborate can pool resources, share investments, and spread risks, allowing for more effective capital utilization and lowering the financial burden of growth projects. This strategy to shared risk offers a buffer and raises the chance of success in new initiatives.

Alliances promote information sharing and learning. firms may learn from one another and get insights into new technologies, best practices, and creative methods by collaborating with firms that provide various knowledge, viewpoints, and experiences. This collaborative learning strengthens organizational skills and fosters a culture of continuous development.

Collaboration with alliance partners frequently results in innovation and faster product development. Organizations can co-create new goods, technology, or services that answer changing consumer requirements and market trends by merging complementary resources and skills. This collaborative strategy reduces time-to-market and increases competitive advantage.

Alliances allow access to common resources and scale economies. Organizations that collaborate can profit from pooled infrastructure, manufacturing facilities, distribution networks, and purchasing power. This offers cost reductions, operational efficiency, and increased market competitiveness.

Strategic relationships can provide access to new technology, intellectual property, or R&D expertise. firms may expedite their innovation efforts and gain a competitive advantage by working with firms that have unique technical developments or expertise. Access to new technology or R&D skills can result in game-changing innovations and market differentiation.

good alliance management necessitates good communication, trust, and goal alignment. It is critical to develop clear governance structures, roles, and duties, as well as decision-making and conflict-resolution methods. Regular communication and collaboration ensure that the alliance stays focused on its common goals and that any obstacles or concerns are handled as soon as possible.

It is critical to evaluate the performance and impact of coalitions on a regular basis. Monitoring key performance measures like as revenue growth, customer happiness, or market share aids in determining the efficacy of collaborations. This review enables firms to make changes, revise strategy, and investigate new possibilities to guarantee the alliance continues to promote development.

To summarize, utilizing partnerships for growth allows firms to tap into complementary resources, knowledge, and market access. Organizations may broaden their reach, cut expenses, promote innovation, and accomplish mutual growth goals by cooperating with strategic partners. These partnerships develop a collaborative atmosphere, allow firms to benefit on shared capabilities, and open up new possibilities for long-term success.

Managing and Nurturing Partnerships for Mutual Success

Establishing successful techniques and practices to develop solid, long-term connections with alliance partners is part of managing and nurturing partnerships for mutual success. To guarantee that both sides extract benefit, achieve their goals, and maintain a pleasant and beneficial partnership, continual cooperation, communication, and mutual support are required. Let's take a slow and easy approach to this concept:

The core of good relationship management is open and honest communication. It is critical to develop clear communication lines, foster a culture of trust, and maintain regular interaction with alliance partners. This enables the flow of ideas, information sharing, and the effective settlement of any difficulties or obstacles that may occur.

Creating a common vision and goals that are aligned is critical for mutual success. Establishing a shared understanding of the partnership's purpose, objectives, and expected outcomes is critical. This shared vision serves as a foundation for collaboration and guarantees that both sides are working toward the same objective.

Regularly evaluating and amending the partnership agreement or contract helps ensure that all parties involved have clear expectations, duties, and obligations. This material serves as a reference and a foundation for decision-making, resource allocation, and conflict resolution.

Implementing performance metrics and tracking key performance indicators (KPIs) enables progress assessment and evaluation of the partnership's impact. This allows both parties to evaluate the efficacy of their collaboration, identify areas for improvement, and make data-driven decisions to increase performance.

It is critical to nurture the connection via mutual support and value creation. Each partner should aim to contribute unique qualities, resources, or experience to the table in order to improve the partnership's total value offer. This might include information exchange, access to networks or distribution channels, or giving assistance in areas where one partner may have a competitive advantage.

Regular collaborative planning meetings and reviews allow both parties to coordinate their plans, discover opportunities, and handle any emergent business difficulties or changes. This collaborative strategy ensures that the collaboration stays dynamic and adaptable to changing market conditions.

Celebrating triumphs and honoring each partner's efforts builds a good and effective partnership atmosphere. Recognizing accomplishments, recognizing milestones, and expressing gratitude for both parties' efforts builds the link and drives continuous dedication to the partnership's success.

Conflict resolution is an important component of relationship management. Disagreements or disputes may emerge during the partnership's duration, and it is critical to resolve them constructively and swiftly. Creating systems for open communication, mediation, or arbitration can aid in the resolution of disputes in a fair and mutually beneficial manner.

Investing in relationship-building activities, such as joint events, training sessions, or social gatherings, helps the partners develop stronger bonds and a sense of camaraderie. Beyond the formal business components, these events give possibilities for human encounters, trust building, and relationship strengthening.

It is critical to examine and reassess the partnership's strategic fit and value offer on a regular basis. Business circumstances change, and the partnership must adapt. Periodic reviews and input from internal and external stakeholders assist ensure that the collaboration stays relevant, aligned with corporate goals, and mutually beneficial.

In conclusion, maintaining and cultivating relationships for mutual success takes constant work, good communication, shared goals, and a dedication to cooperation. Organizations may form strong, resilient partnerships that produce value, promote innovation, and offer chances for sustained growth by creating open lines of communication, keeping a shared vision, nurturing the relationship, and managing disagreements constructively.

Conclusion

Congratulations on finishing this instructive and empowering entrepreneurial journey. You have traveled through the landscapes of vision and purpose, market research, competitive analysis, target customer identification, value proposition building, and creating a sound company strategy throughout this book. You've dabbled with team building, finance strategies, product development and launch, marketing and growth plans, operations management, problem solving, and strategic relationship formation.

Remember that entrepreneurship is a journey, not a destination, as you reflect on the plethora of information and insights you have received. The chapters you've read give a solid foundation, a map, and a set of tools for navigating the volatile world of startups. These concepts and tactics will serve as your guiding lights as you begin on this exciting journey.

Beyond the practical knowledge, though, comes something far more profound: a mindset of resilience, adaptation, and continual learning. It is the realization that entrepreneurial success is determined not just by achieving a certain objective, but also by the capacity to adapt, grow, and accept change. The obstacles you will confront may appear intimidating, yet they are opportunities disguised, encouraging you to push the limits of what is possible.

Always keep in mind that entrepreneurship is a journey of self-discovery, development, and transformation. It is a never-ending pursuit of innovation, quality, and influence. Stepping outside your comfort zone, challenging the current quo, and embracing uncertainty with unrelenting commitment all need bravery.

As you begin your business journey, remember that failure is not the end, but rather a stepping stone to success. Accept failure as a source of development, learning, and resilience. Each failure propels you ahead, honing your talents and fortifying your determination.

Accept teamwork and partnerships, because success is rarely accomplished alone. Look for ways to interact, cooperate, and learn from others. Together, you can do more, develop quicker, and leave a lasting impression that goes beyond the boundaries of your firm.

Above all, feed your entrepreneurial instincts. Allow curiosity to guide you, perseverance to feed you, and passion to propel you. Surround yourself with a network of mentors, peers, and advocates who will inspire and elevate you. Maintain your dedication to your mission and your desire to make a positive change in the world.

As you finish this book, keep in mind that the entrepreneurial path is a continual one. Your newfound ideas and tactics are only the beginning. Continuously seek new knowledge, adapt to evolving trends, and embrace the ever-changing entrepreneurial scene.

As you begin on your business journey, may this book serve as a source of inspiration, direction, and encouragement for you. You will leave an everlasting imprint on the world with every struggle you conquer, every milestone you reach, and every life you touch.

Set out on your own road, courageously and passionately, with your newfound understanding and entrepreneurial zeal. Your trip has only just begun, and the possibilities are limitless.

Believe in yourself, your goal, and the wonderful journey that is business.

Your entrepreneurial drive is eagerly awaited by the rest of the globe. With courage, resilience, and unrelenting drive, seize the chance, make your mark, and mold the future. Your path begins today, and your time has come.

www.ingramcontent.com/pod-product-compliance
Lightning Source LLC
LaVergne TN
LVHW022201200926
848481LV00006B/1810